Praise for *This Monk Wears Heels*

"My friend Kodo is so talented, brave, and graceful. They say to really know someone you must walk a mile in their shoes. Reading his story felt like I had popped on a pair of heels, and it was fabulous!"
Carson Kressley, Emmy award-winning TV personality, style expert, fashion designer, and New York Times *bestselling author*

"Due to the societal diktats, unconscious biaises, and stereotypes, the quest for our own identity is a long journey. Kodo-san's book is a generous, sincere, and moving testimonial that shows you the way to be in line with your own values and to find your inner diamond so that you dare to be who you are and who you want to be. *This Monk Wears Heels* is a warm invitation to live in harmony, love, and peace with oneself."
Sandrine Jolly, Brand President Worldwide, Shu Uemura

"Reading *This Monk Wears Heels* makes you feel like you are in Kodo's makeup chair. He heals your heart, and helps your beauty to shine with pride."
Riyo Mori, Miss Universe 2007

"Kodo's generosity and kindness shimmer across each delightful page of *This Monk Wears Heels*. His story will encourage every heart that longs for deeper, more meaningful connection. Kodo invites readers into the wisdom of Buddhism with such gentleness and skill— a world-class example of offering traditional wisdom in fresh and gorgeously relevant new ways. Religious leaders who are trying to figure out how to invite emerging generations into new conversations take careful note—this book belongs at the very top of your reading list."
Sue Phillips, co-founder of Sacred Design Lab, Unitarian Universalist minister, and an Innovation Fellow at Harvard Divinity School

"Kodo's inspiring and heartfelt book shines just as brightly as he does if you ever see him in person. Kodo takes us on his journey towards self-acceptance, healing, and transformation, demonstrating that sexuality, body-affirmation, and even difficult emotions like anger can all be integrated into a Buddhist path to finding true freedom. His story exudes warmth and honesty, giving us the confidence to look deeply at our own stories, to shine openly in our own rainbow palette of colors, especially when others do not want us to shine. Thank you Kodo for your beautiful offering to the world."
Elaine Lai, PhD Candidate in Religious Studies at Stanford University, co-president of the Buddhist Community at Stanford (BCAS)

"... a jewel of self-discovery, self-acceptance, an̲ ̲ ̲ ̲ ̲ ̲ ̲ ̲ ̲ ̲ ̲ ̲ universal spiritual journey. *This Monk Wears H̲ ̲ ̲ ̲ ̲ ̲ ̲ ̲ ̲ Buddhism can be reconceptualized for our tir̲ ̲ ̲ ̲
Hwansoo Kim, Religious Studies, Yale University

This Monk Wears Heels
Kodo Nishimura

First published in the UK and USA in 2022
by Watkins, an imprint of Watkins Media Limited
Unit 11, Shepperton House, 83–93 Shepperton Road
London N1 3DF

enquiries@watkinspublishing.com

Commissioning Editor: Fiona Robertson
Editor: Sue Lascelles
Editorial Assistant: Brittany Willis
Translator: Tony McNicol
Head of Design: Karen Smith
Design concept: Jösse Pickard
Designer: Kate Cromwell
Production: Uzma Taj

A CIP record for this book is available from the British Library
Printed in Great Britain by TJ Books Ltd

ISBN: 978-1-78678-617-3 (Hardback)
ISBN: 978-1-78678-618-0 (eBook)

10 9 8 7 6 5 4 3 2 1 World Book Night Exclusive

www.watkinspublishing.com

THIS MONK
WEARS HEELS
BE WHO YOU ARE

Kodo Nishimura

WATKINS
Sharing Wisdom
Since 1893

Acknowledgements

Do you know what Kodo means? It consists of two Chinese characters: 宏 (ko) means broad-minded, and 堂 (do) means confident. When I was young, I used to find my name ironic because I was the opposite of that. I was always judging others and myself, and I had no confidence.

Recently, my name has become something of a self-affirmation. I love to live free of prejudice and judgment, celebrating with absolute conviction our worth in the world. It has always been my dream to share my thoughts and stories with people everywhere. Since I was born, I have felt my mission is to inspire others so that we can live in a compassionate society.

Thank you to my Japanese team at Sunmark Publishing for finding me. Thank you to everybody at Watkins Publishing for helping me to deliver my message. Thank you to my precious team who support me. Thank you to my mentors and friends who destroyed my idea of "normal" and allowed me to love who I am. Thank you to my parents for always letting me know they truly want me to be happy. Now it is my turn to share the love and wisdom I've received with the world.

Contents

For anyone who has ever
struggled to be honest
with their heart.

Introduction

• • • • •

I am Kodo Nishimura, a Buddhist monk, makeup
artist, and member of the LGBTQ+ community. I read
sutras—sacred scriptures—as a monk, do makeup, put
on heels, and wear sparkly earrings. From the age of
26, I have been proud to own my sexuality, but while
I was growing up, I hid my true self from the people
around me and lived my life thinking I was something
to be ashamed of. I was afraid of being judged and
humiliated. I felt guilty about being "abnormal"
and concealed my true emotions.

   When I was young, gay people were mostly shown
in the Japanese media as being comical or perverted
in some way. Many of the representations on TV were

of men dressed up as women, being nasty divas and villains. There was nothing respectful or sophisticated about them. The portrayal of LGBTQ+ people as a whole was terrible. Fortunately, this image has been changing in Japan—many people have started talking about LGBTQ+ rights, and, since 2015, in many cities there have been growing numbers of same-sex partnerships.

All the same, because of the Japanese media, the culture, and the society I grew up with, I used to think that my sexuality was something to be ashamed of. However, when I traveled outside Japan, I met people who had overcome this sort of discrimination and who were living confidently. I learned that homosexuality has existed since long, long ago, and was recorded in ancient Roman and Greek times. I also learned the history of LGBTQ+ people, and that there was much homosexuality in ancient Japanese society too. I came to understand that there was nothing wrong with being LGBTQ+.

Nobody can say that it is wrong to be who you are.

My childhood home was the Tokyo temple where my father was a priest. My father was born into a farmer's family. He was the second son, so he was not going to inherit the farm business. When he was five years old, he was taken to Tokyo to a distant relative's temple to be adopted by a couple who did not have children. Even though he was not allowed to choose his area of study, he graduated from university with a PhD in Buddhist studies and is now an emeritus professor.

Ever since I was young, people around me expected me to inherit the running of that temple one day. My friends and other people would really annoy me by asking if I was practicing reading sutras already, and if I would be shaving my head soon. I hated it.

Despite those expectations, my parents never suggested I should take over running the temple. Moreover, as they raised me, they accepted that I enjoyed princess role-play and drawing pictures. When I was little, I loved doing those things. There's a comment from my teacher in the yearbook they made when we left kindergarten. It says that I often taught my classmates how to pretend to be Cinderella. At home, according to my mother, I'd put on her miniskirt and twirl around and around. "Look, I'm a girl!" I'd say. My favorite thing was to dance to the song "Bonjour" from the *Beauty and the Beast* movie.

One day, when I was older and cleaning the house, I accidentally came across an old cassette tape of me singing when I was younger. I was improvising random songs and imitating different languages. Hearing that little me on the tape was a surprise. I was making jokes and I could just tell that I had lots of self-confidence. I had loved myself much more back then. When I was around five years old, I would look at myself in the mirror and sigh, "I am so perfect; how can anybody be prettier than me?" and I completely believed it. Where had that little me gone? The little me that expressed themselves so freely, with absolute confidence?

Thinking back, something inside me changed when I went to elementary school. There, the boys were expected to act as boys and girls were to be girls. People made fun of me for being "girly" and the next thing I knew I'd shut that real me up inside. At school, I was a completely different person to who I was at home.

My elementary and middle schools were OK, because I was able to make friends regardless of gender. I would find friends to play with Pokémon or dolls. During middle school, I had good friends who I would get excited with about Harry Potter.

When I entered high school, the gender contrast was much more obvious. I went to a private school where I did not know anybody, and the culture there was foreign to me. The focus was solely on getting into great universities. I completely closed up my heart. Especially when a classmate called me a "faggot" and I felt so ashamed and offended.

During my high-school years, I was barely able to survive. I was constantly depressed and lost. I was not good at academic subjects, and I was not able to make any friends. Boys got excited about baseball or comedy shows. Girls gossiped and talked about boys. I loved Disney princesses and the idea of studying abroad. Nobody seemed to have similar interests to me. I never found a friend or teacher who truly knew me. I spent those years at high school desperately trying to hide my loneliness—and I said to myself every day: *I'm not a bad person. Why do I have to be so lonely?*

The humiliation and misery really fueled my desire to study English and get away. I found refuge in American culture. I would listen to Mariah Carey, Destiny's Child, and Michael Jackson. I would watch movies like *Charlie's Angels*, *The Princess Diaries*, and *Sister Act*. The characters were authentic, unafraid to show who they were, and taught me to follow my heart.

After graduating from high school, I went to study in the US. Finally, a place where people would accept my unique being. However, now I was faced with feeling inferior because of my ethnicity. My complex about my appearance grew. I began to loathe my eyes, my height, and my quiet personality.

But then something happened that changed my life. When I was 20, I graduated from a language school and college in Boston, and entered Parsons

School of Design in New York. There, the students and teachers around me expressed themselves with pride. Little by little, the old ideas of "normal" that had tormented me were replaced by something much more liberating. This was also when I started to work as an assistant makeup artist.

Up until 2019 I worked as a makeup artist in the US and had the chance to work with many models and celebrities. But even though my life was expanding, I still felt like I was in a cage. Why? Because I hadn't been able to come out to my parents. Ever since I was little, there was an invisible spiderweb hanging over my head. I wanted to lift my head up, but I couldn't. I lived with a nervous fear that if I ever relaxed I'd snag my head on something horrible.

When I was 24 years old and had returned to Japan to start training to be a monk, I made the huge decision to come out to my parents. When I revealed the true me, the spiderweb over my head was suddenly swept away. I could look up and see the stars! It was like jumping—SPLASH!—into a pool of peach soda. My world turned pink and fragrant. My life shot upwards like a fizzy soda bubble.

Since returning to Japan, I've had opportunities to appear on TV and in newspapers, magazines, and other media. I've even been given the chance to speak about my experiences and ideas at renowned universities and global companies, for TEDx Talks, and also at the United Nations.

Right now, I can proudly say I'm happy to have been born the person I am. Yet I spent more than half my life at the bottom of a colorless pit. Perhaps there's someone reading this book who's thinking (like I did once), *I can't even imagine revealing who I truly am. That's only for the few, but not for me. There's no way I'll ever say or do what my heart desires.*

I want to say this to you from my own experience: Yes, I know it is very difficult, but it's your own thinking that limits your life, and that is what I want to help you with in this book.

We are all bound in many ways. We can hide our real selves and camouflage ourselves to look like others.

It may seem like the easier choice, but hiding your true emotions and pretending to be somebody you are not because of the expectations of other people is harder.

Gaining information, meeting people, and traveling freed me to be OK about showing the world who I really am. Now I have friends and family who understand what I am thinking and doing, and who support me all the way. I feel like I have defeated the villain in the movie of my life. Of course, I still get confused and depressed sometimes, but in the process of coming out and finding myself, and getting support from people around me, I have learned various lessons that I hope will inspire you throughout this book. I will also be sharing insights from ancient Buddhist teachings, the spiritual tradition that helps me find my way today.

A passage from the Amida Sutra, a sacred Buddhist text, explains the scenery of the pristine Pure Land. It says that in the pond of lotus flowers, "The blue lotus flower shines in blue; the yellow lotus flower shines yellow; the red lotus flower shines red; and the white lotus flower shines white." This means that each flower shines with its own color and is uniquely beautiful. I believe that each person should also shine in their own unique colors.

Everyone is unique, and that diversity is beautiful.

But, in reality, it can be hard to accept and celebrate each other's differences. So in this book I want to explain how you can share your feelings with others, how you can protect yourself from others, and

"No matter in which
direction I searched, I
could not find anything
more precious than myself.
Thus for us all, our own
existence is the most
precious thing. Therefore
we shall never offend
others for our benefit."

Udānavarga 5:18

ultimately how you can shine in your own colors and be celebrated for yourself.

And here is a secret: the ways of makeup and Buddhism may be different, but the goal is the same. My role is to bring out and protect each person's special colors and help them truly shine!

Today, I'm proud to be unique. I know how tough it is to sacrifice the real you just to live. That's why I'm on your side. I want you to love yourself and live with pride.

To start this self-love, you have to accept yourself and believe in yourself. Because believing in yourself is the first step toward others believing in you. Still, you must find firm reasons to believe in yourself. If you are looking for those reasons, I pray that my experiences and thoughts may be of some use to you now.

My goal in life is to help people to be who they are unapologetically and with conviction. That conviction can come from studying who you are, and also from gaining information: researching history and facts, meeting people, traveling, and expanding your horizons. I want to act as a bridge to help you experience all you need to experience, because that is how I freed myself.

I want to show you how living authentically is feasible and honorable. To those who are like that skirt-wearing child all those years ago—and everyone else—may you all look up to the sky and live your best life!

Never be afraid to be who you are. It's time to be true to you.

1

It's Time to Be True to You

1

It's Time to Be True to You

● ● ● ● ●

You are free to live your life however you decide to. The first step is self-acceptance and self-belief.

I don't think of myself as either a man or a woman. I am both. But during my childhood in Japan, whether I liked it or not, I was treated as a boy. Even now I am an adult, most people consider me to be a man. While my body is male, what is inside does not have a gender.

I don't believe people should be defined as a man or a woman. Their body can be identified as such, but our emotions are ever-changing. The body can be either a car or a ship, but the controller may be whoever! The vehicle does not define the person inside, nor can it define where they should go. If I may say more, even if the body is young or mature, it does not define the maturity of the spirit, and the same can be said of skin color and any other physical differences. We never know what kind of controller there is inside the bodies of others.

Hold on to the steering wheel of your life; don't let anybody else control it for you.

I was born with a male body and it says "male" on my family register, the equivalent of a birth certificate in the West. But I don't identify as male. "So, are you female?" you might ask. Well, I'm not that either. Since I was little I've role-played as Disney princesses, but I've never wanted to change to a female body via sex-reassignment surgery.

When someone asks, "Are you gay, transgender, or queer?" I'm a bit stuck for an answer. In fact, until my mid-20s I considered myself gay. But it seems that "gay" refers to people who identify as male and are attracted to men. I don't feel I fit into that category.

I am not transgender either, because I don't consider myself a woman. The "Q" of LGBTQ+ stands for queer and questioning. I don't feel comfortable being called queer, and I am not really questioning or exploring, so for me that feels a bit weird too, to be honest.

I am a proud member of the LGBTQ+ community, but when I try to precisely express where I fit, I find that I don't belong to any one LGBTQ+ category. I doubt I'm the only person who feels frustrated about that. For example, there was a girl with whom I went to the NYC Pride March who had a girlfriend, and who married a man a few years later. Some people feel comfortable being defined by the term LGBTQ+; however, some people cannot be defined by just one term.

The way I see it, my body is a container that happens to have a gender, but the soul it contains does not have a gender, so I don't think it's accurate to categorize anybody.

Currently, I like to consider myself "gender gifted," because I am able to think and live beyond the expectations based on gender, and provide new or alternative perspectives. "Gender gifted" is a term that I heard somewhere many years ago, and it gave me the power to be who I am. It is all about perceiving yourself with an optimistic viewpoint.

Each person is unique, and each person has their own changing preferences, so I promise myself that when I meet anyone I see them not as male, female, or even LGBTQ+, but just as a single human being right there.

I'm part of the LGBTQ+ community, but I don't really feel a fit for any of the letters. I would like to identify myself as "gender gifted."

People might see you differently because of your physical attributes and conditions. However, we should know that our own awareness of being is what makes us *us*. After all, there is no inferiority or superiority in our awareness. We can only perceive our own awareness, so we can never really compare and rank ourselves to others. That is easier said than done, and I still struggle with this sometimes, but I always come back to the principle of self-awareness. This is the core message of the following chapters, because this understanding can never be shaken—as long as you are aware of it.

And now I want to tell you a little more about the Buddhist path that I have chosen to follow, which sometimes surprises people.

What is a Buddhist monk?

Many people expect monks to be quiet, disciplined, and free of desire, chanting in temples and living minimally. So when I began appearing in the media, I saw comments on social media criticizing me, such as: "Someone who wears makeup and dresses up isn't a real monk." Yet I am a monk. I have trained as a monk, passed all the exams, and am officially licensed. I wear a monk's robes and have learned to chant prayers, and I am now entitled to call myself a Buddhist monk. That is just a fact. A monk is somebody who has been received into the order and who has been given precepts to follow.

What does it mean to be a Buddhist monk? What is the fundamental purpose of being a monk? I consider a Buddhist monk to be somebody who tries to share the Buddhist teachings with others. Just as school teachers are not always perfect when it comes to all the subjects on the school curriculum, Buddhist monks are not perfect either. We can never know if somebody is a perfect monk or not.

I feel that the understanding of what it means to be a monk is often limited. To me, a monk is somebody who seeks to live in a balanced manner and who tries to make the world harmonious. With that in mind, I would like to show how the history and branches of Buddhism support diversity.

Whatever our beliefs, let's improve our understanding and celebrate diversity.

Buddha means "Awakened One"—it is an adjective rather than a specific person. Many versions of Buddha only exist in stories in the sutras, the ancient scriptures. However, a real person called Siddhartha Gautama founded Buddhism in the 4th–5th century BCE.

Siddhartha was born into an aristocratic family in ancient India, but gave up his privileged life to seek enlightenment. After many years, he achieved this and started to take trainees and formed a group of followers. After the passing of Siddhartha, his trainees created books of his teachings using a story-telling format. There are also stories about mistakes the trainees made, which later became a list of precepts. Over time, many other sutras were written in the spirit of Siddhartha, and some were later written in China. The evolution of Buddhism has been dramatic over the centuries. Currently, there are many sutras, and each school of Buddhism reads and believes in different sutras and precepts.

The Buddhist school I studied is Pure Land (Jodo Shu) Buddhism, which was founded by Hōnen in 12th-century Japan. At first only the wealthy benefitted from Buddhist teachings, and the ordinary folk were forsaken. By letting people know that we can all be liberated, the teachings of this school became widely appreciated and the school has flourished, where the original teachings were mostly focused on anecdotes demonstrating the wisdom required to live a harmonious life free of suffering. The Buddhist practices have since shifted their focal point, but what I love about the Pure Land school is that it is rooted in original Buddhism that is accepting and inclusive.

What Buddhism means to me

To me, Buddhism is not something you believe, but something you do. It is not really a religion, but a lifestyle. It consists of a series of life lessons and a way to balance our hearts.

One of the many reasons I admire Buddhism is that it is an old teaching, and yet it says yes to diversity and living your true self. So, why not use these teachings to validate our lives and be happy today?

I am spiritual rather than religious, and I value logical teachings that make sense to me more than blindly following the old Buddhist anecdotes. I prefer to study Buddhism to seek its intention, rather than focusing on detailed examples that are meant to explain core values.

Some people even consider it "science" that measures the universal laws of nature. Since Buddhism is a series of life lessons, instead of only doing what is told, I want to do something that the founder of my school did—to propose an approach that is relevant and necessary in the current era, but whose purpose remains the same: to help people. In this book, I am not promoting Buddhism, but introducing it, especially in relation to how it has shaped my own existence. So if you want to study this path in depth, I would suggest you read other books about the history and teachings of Buddhism.

I also feel that being religious and being spiritual are two different things. You can be non-religious and very spiritual. You can believe or have faith in your own way of thinking, and that is enough for some people. I cannot criticize nor compare any religions, because religion is something that you live with, and I would never want to deny what other people believe in. I don't intend to convert anyone to Buddhism. Even if you follow other religions, I believe that we can all find insights from Buddhist teachings to broaden our views. Buddhism was created to help people, and I want it not to limit me, but to help me go beyond my limits.

I am happy to walk my own path and share the joy with you.

What matters to you?

What matters in life is not what someone else thinks; it is who you believe is the real you. Confidently recognizing what kind of person you are is the fundamental first step toward taking proper control of your life and living as your true self. If you don't dig deep into yourself, you will never quite master yourself. It is about learning how you think, how your body acts. It is about creating your own "how to live effectively" manual, instead of letting others define your life. If we have any complexes or weaknesses, I feel that we should face these to understand why it is so, as acknowledging them will only make us stronger.

As a person who is attracted to men, from my earliest childhood I saw myself as someone who'd suffer discrimination and be made fun of by society. I know that rocky road to the safe place where you can say, "It's OK to live as the real me." I have gone from living a timid life in colorless alleyways to walking true and proud in a ever-expanding Technicolor world!

"Everyone else" doesn't really exist

Because I like men, I thought there was something shameful about me. For a long time I was convinced of it and wouldn't let the real me come out. Being untrue to yourself is like living with constant guilt and never feeling welcomed by anyone. It was extremely hard.

I wish that, as a child, I'd met someone living proudly as LGBTQ+ and saw that there is nothing wrong with being my true self. Then I wouldn't have experienced so much pain. That's the sad thing about not knowing.

When I was a child, people treated me as inferior and I accepted that. I had no choice but to accept a situation where people were called "faggot" or "homo" and bullied. Automatically, I ended up being convinced, telling myself, *Everyone thinks that, so it must be true.*

But actually, deep inside, I didn't accept it. I'd criticize myself, wondering, *I'm not a bad person at all, so why is this happening?* And then I'd give up wondering about that, thinking, *They wouldn't understand anyway.*

The truth is that we each decide how to live our own lives.

I didn't want to give up on living as the real me. Part-way through my life, I chose the path of living with pride: to believe that being LGBTQ+ is not shameful and that we are not inferior.

I'm so glad I could do that. Letting "what everyone thinks" decide how you live is not promising. Because, if my life hadn't worked out, would this "everyone" have helped me? Or would anything have happened by complaining to this anonymous "everyone"?

I know I have to be careful about using the words "everyone," "normal," and "conventional." I don't use them without thinking. This "everyone" that people talk about doesn't actually exist. The words "normal" and "conventional" are merely the measurement of how broad the speaker's horizon is. You realize that there is really no one type of "normal" nor "conventional" if you have traveled around the world and met many people.

Nobody knows about everything or everybody; nor can we ever fully understand what other people are thinking. This life might just be an illusion. What I know for sure are my feelings. So why not use them as a compass to guide your life, given their certainty?

●

Don't listen to what others say; listen to what your heart says

When I was training to be a monk, someone asked me, "How can you convince someone to believe in Buddha if you don't believe in yourself?"

You're right! I thought. When someone truly believes something in their soul, it shows through their words and expression. Words that come from a conviction have the power to move hearts.

Unless you have full conviction, people will not believe you. If there is a tiny dot of anxiety or doubt, people will spot the black dot on the white paper, and start pointing it out.

It was Ángela Ponce, the Spanish representative in the 2018 Miss Universe pageant, who taught me the power of proclaiming: "This is who I am." She was the first transgender woman ever to take part since the pageant began in 1952.

Ángela made world-wide news yet also faced criticism. People said things like, "She'll harm the traditions of Miss Universe," or "She should take part in a transgender beauty competition." Ángela always had the same simple and powerful reply: "*Soy una mujer.*" "I am a woman."

I was at the pageant as a makeup artist and spoke to Ángela in Spanish. "I have always dreamed of Miss Universe, and I once wished that I could compete as a delegate, but I gave up because of my gender," I said.

"So seeing you here competing makes me as happy as if my own dreams had come true!"

She smiled and said, "I have always been a woman. My body has adapted to my soul, and I am a woman. The word 'woman' doesn't just apply to one shape. There are all sorts of women: different races, body shapes, levels of health, and backgrounds. I happen to be a transgender woman. The problem is not that I am a transgender woman, but that society is not educated about diversity."

I felt that we don't need approval from others to be who we are, especially from people who don't know us.

Ángela taught me this: "When the person themselves says it with conviction, criticism from others loses its power." To announce to the world, "This is who I am," a person needs to think carefully to make sure they are ready, and it can be scary to stand out by making that declaration. I want us all to have the strength to speak our truth, and for everyone to respect that truth.

As a transgender woman, Ángela Ponce made history in the Miss Universe pageant. She didn't reach the top 16, but at the end of the competition she had a special walk down the runway with her message being played in a recording of her speaking. I saw her walk so full of confidence and was deeply moved. My eyes overflowed with tears as I saw myself in her.

What made me happiest of all was how the Miss Universe organization had decided she should appear.

I realized that many of the organization's leaders, from many different parts of the world, believed in equality and truth, and it gave me courage.

Yet even though Ángela had won the Spanish competition and been chosen to represent her country, she was criticized by others. It's so sad. I think about where that aggression comes from, and I'm sure that, deep down, it's from the "faceless values" of tradition and custom.

Mostly, when people attack a specific person with criticism and blame, it is based on insubstantial things like historical, cultural, and traditional values, and so-called convention. But don't you think it's sad to be scared into keeping up "appearances" and worrying about conventional values; things you'll discover are completely different in other cultures? Don't you think it's sad not to live as the real you?

Ask that question and I'm sure that many people would say, "You're right!" Still, I understand how some people might not act on that knowledge, even when they understand it logically in their heads, because for a long time I was one of those people. I was afraid of what people would say and how they'd react. I couldn't tell them I was homosexual. Without the experience of meeting people who encouraged me and said, "It's OK. It really is," I'd still be hiding the real me and living in fear. To be honest, there are still times when I'm afraid.

But these days, when I get scared, I encourage myself by saying, "It's OK. It really is!"

If you want to take hold of the wheel, steer your own life, and set out in self-love for a place you love, you must discover the true nature of what traps you and release yourself. Is someone else taking hold of the steering wheel in your life? How do you take back control?

●

Free yourself from the past

I tried remembering the roots of my trauma, and how I came to be ashamed of myself and my sexuality. The instant I discovered its real cause, the trauma disappeared.

I was not able to come out to my parents until the age of 24. My parents studied in Germany and can understand English and German. They often meet people from abroad and they are not the type to have prejudices. As I've mentioned, my father also has a deep knowledge of Buddhist history and he taught sutras in Chinese, Sanskrit, and Pali at university; he also taught me when I studied Buddhism too. But even with parents like that, I felt I couldn't tell them I was homosexual.

Memories from childhood held me back. When I was four or five years old, one of my second cousins, a girl older than me, bought me some glittery rainbow nail polish. I put it on and admired my sparkly nails. I was so happy. But my mom said, "I don't want you to become an adult who does 'that' kind of thing." It wasn't the reaction I'd hoped for. My little mind thought, "Mom doesn't like it when I do girly things."

Then, one time when I was walking with my father in the Asakusa area of Tokyo, we came across someone who was transgender (or "transvestite" as people said back then). My father whispered in my ear: "That person is a man." It felt like he was telling me a secret and I interpreted it as him saying: "It's wrong for men to dress up like women."

Later, he also said, "In order to run a temple, it is essential to have a wife to help take care of many things." I remember thinking: *Does he expect me to get married? That ain't ever happening.*

I think we all have childhood experiences of being hurt by some casual comment, and we don't want our parents to dislike us. That psychological pressure convinced me that I couldn't say, "Look, I'm a girl!" in front of anyone. Instead, I thought, *I like boys and I'm probably going to be discriminated against.*

Much later, I learned I'd misinterpreted my mother's and father's words. But who knows when something might happen that makes you lock your real self away?

Perhaps the same thing happened for you. It's natural when you can't be who you are, and traumatic events don't disappear from our memories easily. I decided that I wanted to resolve this difficulty properly between my parents and me. So, a few years after coming out to them, about which I'll be sharing more later, I asked why they had said what they did.

This is what my mother said: "I don't like nail polish because I feel like the nails can't breathe; I thought that nail polish would be bad for your health. Didn't I give you my skirt when you were at kindergarten? I never told you it was bad to dress up in skirts."

When she said that, I thought, *She's right! One of the photos from when I was little shows me wearing my mother's skirt with a fuchsia* furoshiki—*a wrapping cloth—on my head as long hair. It's right there.*

I learned that when my father said, "That person is a man," he didn't mean anything else by it. He was just commenting on the fact that the person was transgender. However, transgender women were not depicted with any positivity in Japanese society, so I might have extinguished any willingness of my own to live as a transgender woman. If society were completely understanding, things might have been different. Transphobia is something that still makes me afraid to be who I am. I don't want other people to react negatively to me or to be a victim of violence. As of now, I am comfortable with my body, but I would be happy to wake up tomorrow with a female body too.

Anyway, the misunderstandings with my parents evaporated. That's what they were: misunderstandings. But I certainly saw things differently at the time.

When I was growing up in Japan, and later in the US, I was terrified that my parents would hear from someone else that I wasn't heterosexual. I was frightened they'd abandon me if they discovered I was homosexual and scared they'd find out in some indirect way. I made sure not to confide even in close friends. I did not trust anybody.

But not being able to talk about the very core of your identity means you can't be your true self. Isn't it so unfair when you can't accept yourself just because you're different from others? In the end, I believe that the only way to free your heart is to find somebody who you can be yourself with, and tell your stories. Revealing your true self to another person will help to set you free.

Of course, it's not possible for everyone to tell those around them who they truly are. But I believe that telling someone you think will understand can make things easier. There's no rule saying who to tell or when. But if you are ready and decide to tell someone, I support your bravery. And remember that even if the people around you now do not understand you, you can choose your soul family and friends.

The change you seek will come the moment you make up your mind to be your true self.

People don't easily change. But if you run away or give up, nothing will ever change.

●

Separate other people's emotions from your own

After I told my parents I was homosexual, things really did get easier, although I think my father was a little worried at first about how the temple community might react. During that time I appeared on national TV in Japan, where I taught makeup skills to people battling with illness and transitioning as transgender women. I also came out nationally during the program, saying that I had struggled with my own sexuality. One person wrote a letter that said they'd been moved after seeing me on TV. Later, I was also asked to give presentations to other Pure Land school monks and the response was still positive. So it seems my father was reassured in the end.

Online, however, I would read critical comments like, "You're not a real monk. Look at the Thai monks!" Some comments were so off the mark that I instinctively wanted to reply, "What do you know about Buddhism?"

But that's when I had to carefully think, *Why would this person say something like that?* They were only speaking based on what they knew, and that does not mean they were right.

We cannot control the way other people think, but we can try to understand them.

Here's something romantic: during my training as a monk, I had met another trainee who told me that he used to love a man. I was like, *Wow, he might be bisexual!* We got along very well and I started to really like him. I told him that I had feelings for him, but he said he saw me only as a friend. Yet he still asked me to go to Vietnam and Thailand with him. He said he was not sure how he would feel, but wanted us to continue to hang out together.

He had a dream of becoming a film director, but was told by his parents that they wanted him to inherit the family temple and the acupuncture clinic next to it, which his monk father also managed. I think my friend wanted me to persuade his parents to support his dream to be a film director. I did everything I could to support him, from bringing carefully selected gifts for them on my arrival, sweeping the temple, picking up fallen leaves in the garden, and washing all the dishes, to doing ceremonies together, to prove that I could be a good monk doing what I love and being who I am.

I figured that his parents would not know about his sexuality either. When I mentioned that my friend wanted to study in the US, his parents raised an eyebrow. They asked me, "Your parents are also Buddhist priests, right? They said you can do whatever you want in your future? How did they raise you?" Two words—"No way!"—were written on their faces. I wanted to prove that I could study in the US, be free, and still be happy and successful. I wanted his parents to know that a person can fulfil their dreams and still be a brilliant monk as well, so they would support his dream.

At first, his parents welcomed me so much. I was taken to all the good restaurants, hot springs, and local festivals. I was introduced to all their family and friends. I became very close to the entire community. I helped with their household chores and Buddhist ceremonies and events during the day, and we all watched movies together at night.

Because I was still living mostly in the US back then, I would only see my friend during the summer when I went back to Japan. The following year, I was invited to visit again by my friend. I became close to a neighbour of his mother as well. She seemed to be a cheerleader for my friend, somebody who supported him in what he wanted to do.

One day, the neighbour told his mother that I must be a homosexual. It gives me chills to remember this, but all of a sudden she freaked out. It was like a movie. She began to give me the death stare and criticize me for the smallest things, such as not putting my chopsticks on the chopstick rest (which had never happened before). "*Why* are there chopstick rests on the table?" she asked me. I could see her fear and fury that her son might be attracted to men too, which is the last thing she wanted to see happening. She had raised her son to be a monk, and to take care of her later in life. She could not let him be with a guy, nor let him live in a different country. Never!

An emergency red alarm started ringing in my head. Usually I would watch movies with the family, but that night she told me to go to bed right away because they needed to talk about something as a family. I was so frightened. I didn't know if I would wake up alive the next morning. Staying in another family's temple, with somebody giving me that glare, the night seemed even darker than usual. I was unable to talk to my friend, who was going to be sleeping upstairs, so I texted him: "Please do whatever you think is the best for you. I am ready to leave tomorrow so don't worry about me."

"There never was, nor will be, nor is there now, anyone who is wholly blamed or wholly praised."

Dhammapada, 228

The next morning, my friend did not get up until the afternoon. It was so awkward waking up alone and having to see his mother. She told me, "My son is getting married in this temple and having a family. So give up. You have been nice and hard-working, but are you acting this way to convince us that homosexuality is acceptable? Homosexuality is unnatural. It is due to food additives and colorings that your hormones were corrupted. You should read a book about macrobiotics!" She added, "Your mother must have consumed food additives so that you ended up being born homosexual."

I was so shocked I didn't even feel anger then. I struggled to understand how this person could say such things to me. Later, my friend came downstairs and I asked him what they had talked about the night before. He said his mother had learned that I was homosexual, and that it was against the law of nature. He had tried to defend me by saying that she was wrong, but he wasn't able to explain it to her or convince her. He seemed totally lost and helpless.

Finally, he said, "I only see you as a friend, so thank you for the past two years that we hung out."

I thought that if I got emotional and argued back, his mother would have won by making me angry and looking like I really was corrupted in some way. So I just said, "Thanks for all you have taught me."

His father handed me 30,000 yen, which is around $300, saying that it was from the temple for my cleaning work and participating in the Buddhist ceremonies. I said, "No, I don't need it."

He said, "Well, it's for your airplane."

I just said, "Thank you," and I left alone.

On my way to the station, I called my mom crying, and she immediately booked a flight back from Kyushu to Tokyo for me.

I was furious like never before. I had never experienced that much hate toward me because of my sexuality, and it was my friend who had asked me to come over two years in a row, even after I had told him that I liked him. What did I do wrong to deserve to be treated this way, to be told that I was going against both nature and my family?

Afterward, I read the book about macrobiotics that my friend's mother had talked about. It describes homosexuality as abnormal, and claims that when the balance of the body's yin and yang has gone wrong, a person turns to desiring animals and people of the same sex.

For many months, I wondered, *Why does she resent me so much? Why did that person say those things?* Anger took over me, my eczema exploded, and I hated myself even more. I was deeply depressed, and my heart never smiled. I thought about retaliating in the worst ways, but these thoughts only made me suffer even more. I began writing my thoughts in notebooks to help myself analyze what had happened.

> **"In mountain clefts and chasms the streamlets gush loudly, but great rivers flow silently. Empty things make a noise while the full are always quiet."**
>
> Sutta Nipāta, 720

I came to understand that my friend's mother probably felt trapped in the temple, and was expected to act a certain way. His mother had projected her suffering onto me. When her son had been born, apparently she hadn't wanted him to be a monk, but due to the pressure from his grandparents, she had brainwashed herself into believing he would be, and devoted her life to raising an heir for the temple. She was taught to sew robes for the monks and told to stay in the temple to serve the guests. She was not allowed to travel or even participate in activities outside the temple precinct. I remembered that she had only recently been allowed to join local volunteers that helped children with sports, dance, and to play in nature. She was literally trapped in the temple; she must have been lonely and frustrated. I finally understood that it was she who was sad and angry, so how could she allow somebody else to come and go, and be free and happy?

I was eventually able to let go of my anger. I know that I am aware, I am talented, I am loved, and I am free.

I stopped being angry at people who are not happy, because I am not living their lives. When you experience negative emotions from others, your own emotions can be negative too. But I realized that you don't have to accept others' emotions. You can feel pity for them and, if possible, you can try to help them. Because these people are often hiding their vulnerable emotions as well.

What you do have to do is look at the origins of your own emotions.

Sometimes getting angry can make changes, so anger is not all bad. However, constant anger is not healthy. I would use anger as a motivation for improvement, and refuse to stew in it for too long.

"As the dust settles with the rain, so suffering can be settled with wisdom."

Udānavarga, 12:2

"Conquer anger by not getting angry. Do good and defeat evil. Conquer meanness with generosity. Conquer dishonesty with truth."

Dhammapada, 223

●

Why do you feel the way you do?

If somebody else makes you angry, it is because you care. If it wasn't important, you wouldn't get angry.

I have agonized about my sexuality and I have learned to treasure it. My parents are also hugely important to me. They have told me to do what I love and live wherever I want to live. I get angry when things that are important to me are unjustly offended.

I believe that anger originates within us. Buddhism teaches that anger begins with the idea that "I am right," and the three poisons of ignorance, anger, and greed are the root cause of human suffering. We can aim to surpass these by living in harmony with the Noble Eightfold Path (see page 105).

It's so difficult to love and help somebody when we are angry, yet as human beings, we may never be completely free of these three poisons. On the other hand, they can motivate us to do better. Anger and hatred can encourage us to better control our emotions by imagining alternative ways. Ignorance and delusion can inspire us to further study what we don't know.

We are sometimes angry because we are not being entirely honest with ourselves. And the truth is that we are not always right. For example, the other day I got irritated and thought, *This person talks for so long.* When I considered why I was irritated (and I don't always think about this person that way), I realized I was just fidgety because I wanted to go to the toilet! I blamed the other person as I did not want to acknowledge I was angry just because I was waiting to go to the bathroom.

When you endure or suffer, you aren't fully listening to yourself, and can't say why you do it either, so it's easy for anger to arise. After all, it's easier to put the blame on others. Like somebody who was unable to free themselves from suffering and reflected that anger toward me.

Some people are completely bound by the rules of their family or community. Others are forced to study as if there is no other choice. It's understandable that when people with lives of endurance see me—a monk who wears high heels and does makeup—they get angry and say, "That's not a monk!" Because if those people accepted who I am, they would probably start to think, *What are my own values really?* It's natural for people to react with unease to unfamiliar things. For example, when I was younger, my father told me not to wear red pants because they're too loud. Another time, he told me not to wear sunglasses because I could be associated with the Yakuza (Japanese mafia). I thought "Oh, come on! What's the big deal?" but he is right to an extent. When Japan lost WWII, most of the Japanese people were poor. In order to rebuild solidarity, people refrained from showing off wealth and going on vacations. However, today this value can oppress people from attaining opportunities or demonstrating uniqueness.

The Japanese word for endurance— 我慢 (*gáman*) —is actually a Buddhist term. These days it tends to mean enduring things, but the word's literal meaning is "egoistic pride." Buddhist teachings warn against feeling important, getting puffed up, and looking down on others. And endurance truly is a form of arrogance. I've been in a situation where I used up my own time, pushed aside my feelings, and put up with things—all for a particular person. I thought that if I endured, they would understand my value. It really was arrogance because I assumed that person figured "I was right". As a result, nothing changed in them. I started resenting that person, my eczema got worse, and I suffered.

You can't really change anybody else; the only person you can change is you.

I'm sure there will be other times when I end up enduring or suffering. But when it happens, I intend to ask myself, *Are you enduring something you shouldn't?*

●

Learn to listen to yourself

The world still tends to speak of endurance and self-sacrifice as beautiful virtues. How boring for your one and only life to be with little pleasure and full of endurance! (I'm not saying we should be drowned in pleasure either.)

Personally, I don't think it's wrong to avoid pointless suffering so that you can look after yourself. It's OK not to endure, it's OK not to hide your true feelings, and it's OK to show your weaknesses. And it's also OK to do the things you want, express your opinions, and enjoy your life. You should never be ashamed to say what you love. Nobody has a right to deny what your heart is attracted to.

Someone might say, "Isn't it just life not to be free?" Never forget this: you're here and now is what you have chosen. It's not what your parents, your boss, or your friends told you to do. If you just do what someone else tells you to do, you are entrusting your life to others.

Self-destructive thinking—thinking that sees arrogance and self-sacrifice as good—can often steer you away from being true to yourself. I approve of working hard for yourself, but you'd be surprised how often self-destructive thinking lurks behind ideas like, "If only I endure," or "I can't quit while everyone else is working hard."

You know, the thought that "everyone has to be the same" can limit your life and make you suffer. To truly live as yourself, you must draw a line to protect yourself. I tell myself that *There's no need to do what is expected* each time these situations arise and then I pluck up the courage to be true to myself.

You have to decide the course of your own life.

Don't make yourself suffer by using self-destructive thinking to endure things you don't want to do! Loving yourself means protecting yourself. So don't try so hard that you ignore your own heart.

Put aside harmful thoughts

In my school of Pure Land Buddhism, we worship
Amida Buddha, who came into being after the physical
death of Siddhartha Gautama. Amida Buddha is
introduced in the Mahayana sutras, where he says that
if we chant his name then he will guide us to the Pure
Land, which is like heaven. There we can train to be
Buddhas ourselves, and eventually reach enlightenment
and break free of reincarnation—the cycle of rebirth,
where we keep coming back after death to live as
animals, humans, or even starving ghosts or celestial
beings. But there will always be suffering whenever we
lose mental peace. We will always be caught up in the
three poisons of anger, greed, and ignorance. Therefore
we chant and pray that we do not have to come back
to the cycle of life and suffer more.

To meditate by chanting, my fellow monks and I
repeat: *Nam Amida Butsu*. ("I devote myself to Amida
Buddha.") We are taught that we can all be liberated
as long as we chant faithfully even if we are mere
humans who constantly make mistakes. Which is
non-discriminatory and forgiving. I do not expect
you to chant the name of Buddha, because I know
everybody has their own values. So let me introduce my
favorite way to listen to your heart that I think can be
utilized regardless of a person's faith.

Meditate to listen to your heart

When I'm anxious or don't understand something, I ask myself a question: "What is my heart thinking?" And I never close my ears to the answer. To listen to your own heart, write down your thoughts as they come on a sheet of paper. Write whatever comes to your mind, as if your heart is speaking. Once you are able to visualize your thoughts, you will start to see what is preventing you from being free, or what is making you suffer.

1   Sit at a desk or table where you will not be disturbed—if you need to lock the door, do so!

2   Pick a pen that lets you write smoothly, and a blank sheet of paper.

3   As your thoughts bubble up, write them all down For example: *I've started this note but I don't know what to write. Oh well, my family is asking me to go*

on a trip, but I really need to finish my book, so I don't know if I should join them. It might be nice, but this is crunch time, so no mercy, but you know what? Maybe I can still work in the hotel room ...

Just like this; whatever comes into your mind!

4   Stop once you feel like you have written enough.

5   Read what you have written through quietly, and use it to analyze what is currently happening in your life, and what is bothering you. By doing this, you will be able to see your situation from a distant perspective.

6   Repeat this exercise as often as you want. There is no such thing as too little or too much.

RuPaul once said that meditation is what enables you to get off a river, where your emotions are constantly flowing, and climb up a mountain and see the river from a distance. Then you can observe the situation from a different perspective and see clearly. This is what I did to overcome my anger at the discrimination I received over my sexuality. And you know what? You don't even need to write anything down; if you prefer to say your thoughts out loud or tell your friends how you are feeling, that is OK too! I do all of this! It's all about saying what's on your mind without filters. After the clutter is cleared away, honesty peeks out.

Find self-acceptance

What is needed to live with self-love? For me, it is to find reasons to love yourself and to be confident. The process of building confidence is essential, yet most people incorrectly think that confidence is the same as being good at things. Confidence means believing in yourself. But what's necessary so that you can believe in yourself?

Personally, I think it's about knowing what kind of person you are, understanding what you can and can't do, and believing in that fact. In Japanese, confidence is written as self-belief, 自信 (ji-shin), so it does not mean that you have to be good at something, but that you know who you are as a person.

Of course, it's wonderful to be confident about being good at languages or looking beautiful, but the instant someone better than you appears, that belief tends to wobble. Belief in abilities or looks won't support you when you feel down or have problems, will it? So I don't consider those things to be true self-belief. Rather, I think being able to believe in who we are as people, in our personality and way of thinking, is powerful because these will not change no matter who else comes into the room. For example, I know that I enjoy art and music; I know that I can be a good listener; I know I think creatively. These are sources of confidence that do not require any particular skill or ability. Perhaps you don't believe in yourself because you think you're less capable than others? But, you see, confidence isn't just about being better at things.

Even in a tough situation where you think, *I'm no good at anything. I'm mentally exhausted. I don't have the courage to attempt anything*, I'd like to tell you this: Actually, you have the unshakeable awareness that comes from fully understanding your situation right now. Nobody is perfect. It's a wonderful thing to be able to recognize your situation, understand it, and accept yourself as you are.

When you know who you are and can accept that with positivity, you realize that it's pointless to compare yourself to others.

That's an unshakeable source of confidence in any situation. And I'm sure it will make living life easier!

Be honest with yourself

Be realistic about what you're good and not good at.
That's the first step. You need a "cannot-do" confidence,
as well as a "can-do" confidence.

I think that belief in what you're good at, or not good
at, is a kind of confidence. For example, my "can-do"
confidence is related to languages and art. I'm still having
fun studying English and Spanish. When I talk in those
languages people tend to be surprised and praise me, so
I guess I have more ability than most. I make use of that
"can-do" confidence by memorizing greetings in many
other different languages to say hello to people from
those countries. People are happy when I talk to them
in their own language and there's an instant rapport.

On the other hand, there are lots of things I
am confident I "cannot do," like sports and some
academic subjects. I'm not good at history, for
example, but I realized that if I know something
about someone's country and its history, I can better
understand what is happening in the world today.
So now when I'm training at the gym I listen to a
fun podcast series about the history of the world
and religion. I've read manga about history in the
past and didn't remember that at all. But with this
podcast I can have fun finding out about the history
and cultures of the world and enjoy it just like I'm

"Deep wisdom, acquired
skills, learning to be
disciplined, brilliantly
used words—these are
happiness."

Sutta Nipāta, 261

listening to the radio. My vague knowledge soon started to come into focus, while my feelings of unease and inferiority gradually faded away. I was really reminded how important knowledge is.

Once you accept what you're not good at, you can look for other ways to get them done. That's why I think it's important to admit a "cannot-do" confidence.

Don't think you can do it all yourself. Everyone has different abilities, so accept what you can't do and ask for help.

It's crucial to understand what you can and can't do, and to acknowledge your capabilities without deluding yourself. Society expects us to know things and to be able to do things to a certain degree, so unless you accept the fact that you cannot do some things, you'll start hiding and denying your weaknesses. At the other extreme, when you are praised all the time, you can become needlessly proud and vain. And that conceit and vanity will only hold you back from living your truth too.

There are still plenty of things I'm not good at. I'm not good at understanding manuals for computer software such as excel and photoshop. All I need to do is contact someone who seems good at that stuff and ask. Then there's rarely a problem.

Different people are good and bad at different things, so why should you take on everything yourself? When you have "cannot-do" confidence and rely on the help of others, the things you can't do turn into things you can!

I now like tidying, but when I returned to Japan in 2019, my old room was a jumble of stuff: manga from when I was at school, letters from classmates, broken items, notebooks from old classes. I asked myself a question: *Could someone who can't even tidy their own house feel beautiful and successful?* Of course, the answer was no. *I need to do something about this*, I thought. So I took three tidying-up lessons from someone I decided would be the perfect teacher for me. That person was a top apprentice of Marie Kondo, the author of *Spark Joy*.

Now all my things are carefully sorted out and I can even say that I live surrounded by things that spark joy. Success! Even as I write this, more than a year after I took lessons, my closets and drawers are beautifully organized. I keep my room tidy enough for anyone to come over and take a photo anytime!

I'm not embarrassed by things I can't do and I don't hide them. I listen carefully to advice from experts and then, after they teach and help me, I can do it too.

But I think the results depend on the teacher. That's why I take great care over finding someone who can teach me well. My way is to spend less time worrying and more time looking for a good teacher. If the teacher does not make you feel that you are actually improving, I would move on to the next teacher. There are many people who call themselves professionals but are not really qualified to be considered as such. (Sorry, but I'm just being honest!)

●

Flip your weaknesses into strengths

I've said that knowing what you can and cannot do gives you confidence. But I believe working on everything with positivity—your strengths and weaknesses—is the key to finding the true you. When you get better at the things you're good at, it's an obvious improvement. Meanwhile, even those things you thought were weaknesses can become attractive features when looked at differently.

I used to dislike the way I speak. People would tell me that it made them feel sleepy! For a long time I thought I had to correct it. But, instead of making some futile attempt to make my voice snappier, I changed my thinking. I decided to make my voice more "relaxing," and that became an aspect of who I am. Soon my friends told me things like, "Nobody can soothe people with their voice like you," or "It's calming; you should read bedtime stories." I began to think of my voice in a positive way—as a strength rather than a weakness.

I also used to have a complex about my almond-shaped eyes, but I've given up on applying glue to make a double eyelid so my eyes seem bigger. Instead, I use my own eyes' distinctiveness by extending my eyeliner sideways and making my eyes look even sharper. My eyes have become something I can use to say, "This is me!"

Instead of chasing some far-off ideal, accepting what looks good on me has made me confident. Not Barbie, but Asian beauty!

In the same way that some Asian people long for a big-eyed biracial look, some people in Europe and North America admire the sharp, mysterious look of long and almond-shaped Asian eyes. When I was hanging out with my Spanish friends, one of them even said, "I want to get facial surgery so that my eyes are narrower, and my nose is lower." At the time, I was completely shocked that somebody wanted to have surgery to look more like me.

I had one specific idea of what beauty looked like, but there are so many types. The decision to appreciate it is

The compliment battle

Struggling to love yourself? I'd like to share a fun game that helped to build my self-esteem. It's what I call the "compliment battle." I was unable to find anything that I liked about myself, so I asked my friends, but in return, I would name good things about them too, which was much easier than identifying things I liked about myself.

1   Find a trusted friend or partner who won't say anything to traumatize you.

2   Think of ten things that are good about each other. This might include some physical attributes, their sense of fashion, their voice, their scent, or positive aspects of their personality.

3   Take it in turns to share your compliments! For example, you might say: "I like your humor," "I like when you write nice emails," "I love your earrings today," "I love when you wear red lipstick."

You may find that it's quite challenging to identify ten positive things about yourself, but that's what's good about this exercise. The other person will be looking hard at you, and you at them, and you will both find good things about each other that you wouldn't have found for yourself.

If you play the compliment battle with five or so friends, there will be things about each of you that multiple people praise. With some of those, you'll think, *Of course they're saying that, because I work hard at it.* But you'll be surprised at some of the other compliments and think, *I had no idea people thought that about me!* Either way, when people tell you objectively about your good points, it's a gigantic boost.

For example, my friends all told me, "Kodo, your head is such a beautiful shape," and, "The way you move is so elegant." When I was doing my monk's training, even a teacher who was a nun had said, "The way you carry yourself is so gentle and graceful, Kodo." Yet when I was at school, I was put down for the way I moved. "You run like a girl," they'd said, so I tried to hide my graceful movements. Now it made me so happy to be praised for something that came naturally to me.

You may assume, "This is just how I am," but perhaps there's a positive aspect hidden somewhere? How about trying something like the "compliment game" to see if you can uncover those good points?

up to me. I don't want to restrict my idea of beauty, when I could change my prejudice in a way to love myself. I want to adopt a broad-minded sense that being unique is also beautiful, and apply it to myself too. When I started thinking like that, I was able to change.

Of course, I didn't suddenly start loving my eyes. I practiced doing makeup again and again, noticed things, and kept experimenting. Once I'd perfected eye makeup that let me love my eyes, I started to love my eyes without makeup too.

> "The one who protects oneself protects others as well, so protect yourself. These people will not be harmed, and are wise."
>
> Anguttara Nikāya

It's not the ideal I had in mind at first, but once I accepted a way of being that was natural for me, I realized that it suited me. It feels very comfortable to be the real you, and when you feel comfortable, you love yourself. Being able to love myself makes me happier than anything. I did not have to keep trying to be somebody else anymore; I was already complete!

There was once a time when I couldn't love myself, maybe because I was pessimistic about my sexuality. I had low self-esteem and complexes about my looks. I got depressed when I looked at mirrors or photos. After trying lots of things, now I can truly say I love myself!

It's not a sin to enjoy your life. If you don't live in each moment, you'll end up missing your chance to have a fun life. We can only live in this moment, so please don't postpone the things you enjoy. If you wait to be happy, you will never be happy. So celebrate today! I try to live knowing that everything can be lost one day. I can be sad thinking about it, but that is the best way to prepare for the future and enjoy the moment.

We must work hard for the sake of our future lives; I don't deny that. It's the cycle of birth, death, and rebirth. But what a waste not to enjoy our present lives. "One life" has become my favorite quote, especially since studying Buddhism and reincarnation. Ironic, right? I ask myself: *Is there anything that I am postponing that I actually want to do? Should I go skydiving tomorrow?* The answer may be no, but it is good to ask myself so that I have no regrets later.

2

Find Your
Own Path

Find Your
Own Path

● ● ● ● ●

*When you decide to live your truth, you will
realize there are many people who love you
just the way you are. It's time to go find them.*

Allies appeared when I came out. Unless you share your
true self with those around you, nobody will be able to
support you. If you hide yourself from the world, you
will not discover what it can offer. Even Siddhartha
Gautama did not achieve enlightenment by staying at
home. He traveled the world as a spiritual seeker.

Until I graduated from high school and started
living abroad in places like Boston and New York, I'd
thought, *I like men, so I can't make friends.* But looking

back as an adult, I think I'd just decided, *I like men, so everyone will reject me*. That turned into my reality and caused me sadness.

In fact, there was a guy at school who spoke like a diva and who had plenty of friends. He had a crew cut and glasses, was an excellent student, and was always at the top of the class. I guess other people respected him for that. He would giggle with all the girls and was very unapologetic about who he was. He was the complete opposite to me at that time.

With hindsight, if I'd had the courage to be my true self at high school, my situation could have been different. But I decided I wouldn't be accepted. Of course, not everyone would have understood and perhaps some would have rejected me. But I think just as many would have accepted me. Yet I made excuses: *I'm not smart like the crew-cut guy, so they won't accept me*. I classed everyone as enemies, assuming they wouldn't understand me. It seems obvious now, but would these people I'd seen as enemies have opened their hearts to me or helped me?

If you always hide your true self and run from those you think are enemies, you will end up pushing yourself into the shadows.

Of course, there are still tragic cases of discrimination happening around the world, so we have to be very careful and protective of ourselves when it comes to expressing our uniqueness. In my case, I thought I would be discriminated against, and that was probably true at the time. However, the world is changing and people are learning to respect our differences, particularly thanks to how values can now be shared globally on the internet.

Let me tell you a little more about the journey that brought me here today. Here is what happened when I was young and how I used to feel as my younger self.

How did the journey of your life begin?

If you think of life as a journey, you can return to your childhood to discover who you were when you were little and setting out on your way—before you started to hide your true self from the world.

I have already told you about the photo that shows what kind of child I was. I'm wearing my mother's dress and I am cuddling Búbulu, a soft toy who still sleeps in my bed today. I was the kid who looked like the Little Red Riding Hood.

My kindergarten had lots of skirts with elasticated waistbands for playing dress-up. A friend showed me how I could wear a skirt on my head and pretend to have long hair. I adored letting my new "hair" flow and my skirt swish around.

Apparently, I'd often tell my mother, "Look, I'm a girl!" When we went into town, sometimes people would say, "How cute she is." But each time, Mom would reply, "No, he's a boy." I remember being disappointed when I heard her and thinking, *What? That's not really right.*

The other children would play dodgeball in the kindergarten yard or school yard, but I never once thought about joining in. I was scared of the ball hitting my fingers. It was much more fun to stay inside by myself and draw pictures of Ariel from *The Little Mermaid* or Sailor Moon, the manga superheroine. I loved stories about women getting together to go up against evil. *Sailor Moon* and *Charlie's Angels* were like that.

When I was in kindergarten, I didn't have the magic batons and fairy sticks you could buy in toy shops at the time, but sometimes that kind of paper-crafted kit came free with magazines, and my older cousin (who was 19 at the time) helped me put together my own. I loved my cousin and wanted to marry her when I got older. I wonder if it was just because we had fun playing together. Or was it because I thought marriage was only between men and women? I didn't really understand the nature of my sexuality when I was small. The little me would proudly say, "Look, I'm a girl!" But as I got older, I didn't know what to call myself anymore.

From the start of elementary school, I loved wearing denim overalls. They have an androgynous look, so someone like me (neither a girl nor a boy) could wear them and not worry at all. When I was young, I would play dolls with girls, and I would go cycling and play Pokémon with boys. Gradually, I started saying things like, "I don't like boys," and "I don't want to play with boys." It made my mother worried that there was something wrong with her child-rearing. She had books on her shelves with titles like *How to Raise a Child*. I noticed and decided it was my fault she had to read those books. (Even though there was nothing wrong with me!) It made me very sad.

During my third year of elementary school, we visited a special education center. While my mother consulted staff, I played the video game *Street Fighter* with a lady who worked there. I loved that. In order to make me better at sports, and possibly be able to play with other boys, I also had sports lessons as a child— but I would really fall in love with the male instructor instead. I would literally cry with unrequited love, because I knew he was a heterosexual guy. This always happened to me: whenever I fell in love with boys at school, I was sure that they would either see me as crazy or creepy. It was such a hopeless feeling.

During the school swimming classes, I was unhappy and embarrassed when I had to wear a boy's bathing suit. I felt many things to be unreasonable. Even when I was three years old at kindergarten, I hated to show my body to others. I went inside the curtain and changed there.

As I got older, I didn't know what to call myself anymore. I used to say "Kochan." It is a short version of Kodo, with "chan," which is a Japanese honorific for cute people. This was like a child calling themselves their own name. I didn't want to use the Japanese word for "I"—*Watashi*—that girls and adults use, because it was unnatural for a little boy to say. Japanese has many different first-person pronouns that indicate things like gender, age, and status etc. But I didn't want to use the "I" words—*Bóku* or *Olé*—that boys and men use either. With no good options, I chose a neutral and standoffish word for "I" from western Japan—*Uchi*. It was a struggle to talk about myself because of the gender-defining language. All these uncomfortable things attempted to divide me into the categories of men and women.

●

What did you love when you were little?

When I was younger, I didn't see the point in studying because I was sure that I was never going to use many of the things that we were taught at school. I used to scribble over my homework with a pencil and had to stay behind after class alone to do more work.

Even after moving up to middle school, I couldn't care less about study. "Who uses these formulas when they are an adult?" I'd say. Or, "How come the English word 'friend' is spelled like that when it would make more sense to spell it as 'frend?' It does not make sense." I had plenty of doubts and no interest in studying. But during the summer vacation of my first year at middle school, when I was about 12 years old, my mother and I went to Hawaii ... and I fell in love with the place and caught the English-learning bug.

My mother is a pianist and one of her piano students, who lived near us in Tokyo, was studying in Hawaii. Her name was Mizué. She looked so stylish and cool when she appeared on her scooter! She held a cellphone in one hand and chatted with her friends: "Hi! What's up?" She translated the restaurant menu for us and confidently ordered in English. Her English was often complimented by the locals. I watched and thought, *I want to live like that*. And I truly wanted it. From then on, my goal was to study in Hawaii.

And then something incredibly lucky happened. In the second year of middle school a temporary English teacher came to our school, just for a year. She was a Japanese woman who'd grown up in Hawaii. She was so lovely, with beautiful English pronunciation and a cute brunette ponytail that curled up at the end.

One day, she suggested our whole class write exchange diaries in English and share them with her. Exchange diaries are notebooks that friends share and take turns to write in. Most kids quit after about two weeks, but I was totally set on studying in Hawaii so I made sure to write in my journal every day, even after I was the only one left still writing one. Even the teacher's handwriting was delightful and she made corrections in fuchsia ink. I checked my mistakes each time, then wrote more. Thanks to that, my English class marks improved enormously.

I had a different English teacher during the third year of middle school, but I asked the teacher if I could keep writing my journal. Thanks to my English grade, I was able to get into a high school a little above my level!

Every life has dark days

Sadly, for me, the high-school gates were the entrance to hell. There I found myself struggling with study, and my social life hit a dead end. It was a private high school so none of my old friends were there. I was plunged into a bleak and gloomy age of darkness and loneliness. Boys got excited about baseball, soccer, and TV comedy. The girls talked about makeup and fashion, or chatted happily about the boys. At middle school, I'd been able to join the girls' group, but it felt different there. The boys were boys and the girls were girls. Clearly separate. As I wasn't a boy or a girl, I had nowhere to go. I would spend recess utterly alone, without anyone I could call a friend in my class.

Because I was scared that someone might notice I was homosexual, day after day I didn't speak to anyone. But I didn't want my classmates to think I was a loser either. Each lunchbreak I would casually leave the classroom as if I had somewhere important to go. Then I'd just walk aimlessly around the school building.

Not surprisingly, I started to hate going to school and kept being late. But if you didn't have a legitimate excuse for being late, the teacher would get mad. So, I'd beg for an official excuse slip they give at Japanese stations when trains are late. I just wanted my time at school to be as brief as possible, so every day I prayed for the train to be delayed. I even seriously thought about picking up two slips on the 13th of the month and changing the date on one to the 18th.

The teachers were focused on getting the students into good universities, so they were strict with us and said we had to study ten hours a day. The students were always concentrated on the entrance exams. So when I

Time-travel to discover who you really are

As I grew older, my identity and personality became confused by the values and expectations of society. I believe that the qualities we acquire after we are grown up should not be the core of our being; the soul that we are born with should. I believe that we are our genuine self when we are young, which is why remembering your childhood can help you to find out who you are. It's time to travel back to your childhood years ...

1   Ask your parents and old friends what kind of child you were.

2   If you can, visit the neighborhood where you grew up as a child, and remember how you used to feel. Go to your old kindergarten, playground, and other such places.

3   Look at photos from when you were young.

4   Remember how you used to play, and think about why it was so fun for you.

I've mentioned how I used to play with dolls—I loved how different dresses would make my dolls look like they had different personalities. I also loved dressing myself up in pretty dresses, trying on various materials and accessories, as it made me feel like I had become somebody different. Things I also loved doing included drawing characters, making up stories, and performing my own musicals. So I can now see that I have always been a person who likes to create things, express different identities, and tell stories. I feel that these qualities really lead to who I am, and I can be even more powerful when I am aware of what I love doing. So remember this and retrieve your authentic personality too. I think your young self can encourage you to be your true self!

was in the art class, the other kids would make fun of me for making an effort in drawing. There was no exam in art when applying for university, so why work so hard? Instead, the students spent the art class chatting and killing time. The art teacher would be surprised at what I had drawn and ask me, "Did *you* draw this?", and that was the best compliment. I was proud and said, "Yes, and I can do more!" I would ask for more assignments and would draw on my own outside of class. Unfortunately the art class was only for a year, and the second-year curriculum focused on those subjects that would be tested for university entrance. How sad! People made me feel like what I love and do well at is worthless, but I don't think we should study only the subjects that will be tested.

It is not wrong to enjoy what you love.

Suffering is part of the journey, not the destination

I'm not going to lie to you—my school years were a difficult and lonely time, but I guess they helped pave the way for me to become who I am today. I learned about suffering not by reading about it, but by actually experiencing it.

Buddhism accepts that suffering is a part of the journey of life and describes eight kinds of universal suffering. These include the four sufferings of birth, aging, sickness, and death, which we cannot avoid because we are human. There are also these kinds: the suffering of having to part from people we love, the suffering of having to meet with people or situations we hate (which was me in high school), the suffering of being unable to obtain what we desire (also me in high school), and the suffering arising from the five components that constitute our body and mind: matter, sensation, perception, mental formation, discernment.

So just being alive means suffering! Even when I was older, more comfortable with myself, and working as a makeup artist in the US, suffering continued to be a part of my life. When I did not have jobs as a makeup artist, I used to think that *I was not talented or skilled enough*. Then, when I started to get a little bit busier, I would think *I want to be better and more successful*. And when I was super busy, I would think, *Why do I have to work so much?* It was too overwhelming and I wanted to take breaks. It is too easy to look at our lives and only see the negatives and the suffering.

Many of us cannot escape from thinking about things, making judgments, and getting caught up in suffering. It can help if we change our understanding. Sometimes this means challenging ways of thinking and being aware of our situations; other times, it may mean making a move and finding somebody who understands you and proposes alternative ideas.

●

Seek out your true family

One day, when my class were cleaning the classroom (something Japanese students often do as part of the school day) and I stood facing the blackboard getting ready to go home, I heard a voice behind me. "That kid Nishimura. He's a homo, right?" In that instant, my blood froze. *It's all over. I'm not even the least bit friendly with him. I guess people can just tell*, I thought.

I pretended not to hear and desperately tried to look indifferent, but inside I was like one of those plastic bags people use with a vacuum cleaner to compress duvets. The air was sucked out of me and I shriveled up smaller and smaller. What attitude should I adopt at school tomorrow?

You know, if someone calls me homo, they are only saying the truth. But back then, I didn't have the strength to say, "Yes, that's right. I am a homosexual." I was afraid, so I kept silent. I felt

"Let your heart be the torch.
Follow where it directs you."

Mahāyāna Mahāparinirvāna Sūtra

overpowered by a society that appeared to disregard the LGBTQ+ community.

Even if a million people think something is right, they might all be wrong. You might be the one in a million who knows what is actually right.

In the end, it was English language school and a gay chat room that saved me from a friendless and colorless world. When I told my parents I'd like to transfer to high school in the US, they replied, "Anything but that." And they added: "Considering your school grades, how can you hope to pass the exams in English?" Still, dropping out seemed too much like giving up, so I didn't want to do that either. It was like I was hemmed in on all sides with no way to solve my problems. But it was the English I'd learned that saved me. I found somewhere to be myself during my high-school years: an English-speaking gay chat room on the net. This was a place where kids in the same situation as me gathered. It was the only place I could share my real feelings without hiding them, but only in English!

Although users lived in different countries, such as Greece, Portugal, Russia, the Netherlands, China, the USA, Puerto Rico, and Uruguay, we were all teenagers. We talked, shared our LGBTQ+ worries, and gave each other support; things like, "My parents said that being gay is wrong," or "When someone asks you which girl you like, what do you say?" Without the gay chat room I'm not sure how I would have survived those three years of high school. That is where I felt like I was being heard. I used English dictionaries to chat, otherwise I would not have been able to be honest and talk with anybody. It was a vital tool for me. I could not insist that the word "friend" should be spelled "frend" anymore. I would have no friends speaking like that.

I immersed myself in English in the real world too. Since I had no evening clubs to go to or friends to hang out with after school, I went to conversation class and improved my English instead. It was so refreshing and eye-opening to talk to teachers from all around the world. I would talk about Destiny's Child with an American teacher, and I would learn about Maori people from a New Zealander lady. I learned that there was a whole world waiting for me to discover, where the teachers did not expect me to study ten hours a day and none of my friends would exclude me because I love drawing.

Every day, my routine became school, English class, home, gay chat room. I was always listening to music, too. Mariah Carey, Beyoncé, Michael Jackson, Janet Jackson, and many more. I would sing along, reading the lyrics. I was starting to understand and recognize empowering messages against discrimination and stigma relating to sexism and racism. This was not something that many Japanese singers sung about. Not surprisingly, my high-school English scores were extremely good.

Because I loved art, I even thought about art school as the next step after graduation. Outside high school, I joined an art class to prepare for art school, but was stunned at how much better than me the other students were at sketching. The entrance exam for art schools in Japan mainly consisted of sketching from life. During the class, I would get dizzy drawing for hours and hours, and I asked myself, *Why do I have to draw realistic objects when I could just take photos? What is the point in doing art that does not convey a message?* This approach did not make sense to me. I wanted to use my imagination and creativity. I decided that all that sketching to pass the entrance exam wasn't for me and dropped the idea of going to art school in Japan.

The only thing left was my English ability. At middle school my goal had been to study in Hawaii, so I decided that I wanted to study art in English in Hawaii. Then I joined a cram school where I focused on my English. The advisor there told me that if I wanted to study art, I had to go to New York. I thought New York looked like a place of opportunity and somewhere that might accept me. I remembered movies like *Chorus Line* and *The Lion King*, and I dreamed of going to see musicals. *Perhaps I could make friends there. Perhaps I wouldn't feel so left out.* Those thoughts got stronger and stronger until I decided to leave Japan and study in the US with sparkles in my eyes.

Don't expect anything to change if you won't

My cram school in Japan had connections that supported students who wanted to study abroad, and one affiliated school happened to be in Boston. So, I started college there. It was suggested that I study in Boston for two years and then transfer to a school elsewhere. The advisor said that it would be easier to transfer to New York if I was in a state close by.

I thought if I went to the US, everything would change. But the reality was totally different. I'd hoped and expected to find somewhere to be myself, but actually I couldn't make American friends easily. I started to compare myself to people of different ethnicities as well. Many of them were much taller than me, with beautiful faces, and I felt inferior.

My standard of beauty at that time was determined
by the size of somebody's eyes and their height. I was
seeing myself through the lens of Japanese aesthetics.
I was also shy, which discouraged me from speaking
to people, so I blamed my self-hatred and loneliness
on my Japanese ethnicity. *I can't be accepted even here*,
I thought, and I became depressed.

Then, I read some incredible news. The delegate from
Japan, Riyo Mori, had won the 2007 Miss Universe
competition. *How could an actual Japanese person triumph
at a world-famous beauty contest?* I wondered. I was in
total shock. *Japanese people can be accepted around the
world!* I thought. From that time on, I couldn't take my
mind off Riyo, and when I next went back to Japan,
I found a book about her triumph. At first I hesitated
to buy a book that aimed to teach women how to be
beautiful. I felt like I was buying a racy magazine, but
I was ready for any humiliation. As I approached the
cashier, I worried that the clerk would notice that I
might be homosexual or that a friend from middle
school would spot me, and would ask why I was
buying a book about beautiful women. Well, nothing
happened. I read the book in three hours non-stop
and it was life-changing!

Many things in that book resonated deeply with me.
One passage said: "You might think that in order to be
considered beautiful, you must have blue eyes, blonde

hair, and long legs, but that is not always the case. Most Japanese people have lustrous hair, smooth skin, and youthful willowy bodies, and these are considered beautiful outside Japan." And another explained: "Long and narrow eyes can be brought out with eyeliner and mascara while dark eyes stand out from a distance, which can emphasize serene Asian beauty." And: "Japanese people's humility, ability to show consideration, and diligence are rough diamonds that people from other places find hard to match." It seemed there was hope for me to feel beautiful!

There were lots of dance students at the college in Boston that I attended. These girls were tall and slender, blue-eyed, had great posture, and looked beautiful even just dressed in sweatshirts. *These girls are the actual models for Disney princesses*, I thought. But even though that had been my ideal of beauty, I now realized how I'd only been seeing beauty through a perspective that was heavily influenced by society that tended to idealize Western looks.

It wasn't being Japanese that had stopped me from being accepted. But if not that, then what? Why did I have that belief?

In the same way, we all have beliefs that hold us back: what are yours?

Question your beliefs

I thought a homosexual person could never be accepted in Japan. And in the US, I felt inferior because of my narrow eyes, eczema, and short legs. But then Riyo Mori appeared—a Japanese Miss Universe. What was going on? It dawned on me that I'd been thinking about things the wrong way. Bit by bit, my conception of normal started to expand.

At about the same time, I visited a church in the center of Boston where they had a group for LGBTQ+ youth. I made my first offline gay friends there. It was weird for me to visit a church since I was not familiar with the religion, but it did not matter. I started talking with a guy whose family came from Barbados. He explained how he was unable to come out to his family, and how homosexuality was not welcomed in the Caribbean islands. Even though I was learning how American youth were much more open, I was still struggling to come out. And I was also learning about severe cases of discrimination that happen in other parts of the world, even worse than in Japan.

I remained scared that students at my school would find out I was homosexual so I tried to avoid their company as much as possible. But I did find one female friend. There was a girl called Eri from Japan who I clicked with. We were so close that we chatted for about two to three hours everyday. We'd pour out all our complaints about dormitory life: There were loud parties every weekend, the building shaking with the sound of the loud bass. The dormitory heads were two young men who, instead of stopping the parties full of underage drinkers, organized parties themselves. Both Eri and I were annoyed, and we suddenly thought, *Let's get out of here and share a room together!*

Even though I'm not attracted to women, I have a male's name and body. *Perhaps Eri's parents will worry about her sharing a room with a male?* I thought. *I have to come out to her.* I've always hated it when things aren't done properly. Before anything else, I had to make sure that Eri's parents didn't worry.

So, I decided to come out for the first time to my friend. I worried about when to tell her and my heart was pounding away during our long telephone chats, and my hands got shaky and so cold. Then, one evening, when Eri sounded like she was getting sleepy, I thought, *Now's the time!* I blurted out: "Eri, I'd like you to tell your parents not to worry about sharing a room with me, because I'm homosexual."

But she just replied in her usual tone of voice, "OK, I see. Goodnight then."

What an anticlimax! I was even worried she'd have forgotten by the next day, so I had to check: "That thing I said last night ..." But, of course, she remembered!

With my secret out in the open, I felt totally refreshed. You can't imagine how happy I was that my coming out hadn't altered our friendship at all.

●

Once you have taken a baby step, the rest becomes easier

I chose Spain for my first vacation abroad away from my parents and planned the trip by myself. I'm a big fan of the Japanese idol pop group Perfume, and during my three years of high school, I often visited a Perfume fan site made by a webmaster in Barcelona. So I decided to meet up with him there.

The webmaster showed up with more than ten of his friends, which surprised me. I ended up sharing a meal with these Spanish superfans of Japanese idol pop singers. One of the fans was an ex-boyfriend of the webmaster, who came with his current boyfriend. Awkward! The next day, they took me to famous sightseeing spots like La Sagrada Familia and Park Güell. That's where I got to know the couple who would change my life: Chechi and his partner Kami. They are still two of my most precious friends. From the moment we met, we fit together like jigsaw pieces, whether it was laughing at gay in-jokes or chatting about fashion and other guys.

"Even if it is important
to others, do not give up
what you are tasked to do.
Realize your goal and focus
on your task."

Dhammapada, 166

Meeting Chechi and Kami turned my ideas upside down and fabulous Spain obliterated my old attitudes. (By the way, Chechi is a nickname for Sergio, and Kami is an online nickname for Roger.) I did not have to hide anything, because they were people just like me. Up to that point, I'd never had friends to laugh with and with whom I could share anything. I couldn't believe there were actually people on this earth that I could get on so well with! It was a total shock.

Chechi and Kami were gay, but their attitude toward their sexuality was totally different to mine. They would hold hands in the streets and kiss in public. At first, I was scared they would be stabbed by somebody, but nothing really happened. When I had to leave Spain, I cried like a baby—remember the suffering of having to part from people we love? It was like I was losing the most precious people in my life, people I could be honest with for the first time. On the airplane, strangers kept asking me if I was OK in Spanish.

I missed Spain so much that I decided to go back during the winter break. This time, I stayed with Chechi at his family home. One day, he and Kami suggested, "Since you've never been to a gay club, let's go this weekend. We'll come back tomorrow morning."

I was really worried. How would Chechi tell his parents? But he came straight out with it and told his mom, "We're off to a gay club. We'll be back tomorrow."

His mom said, "Wait a moment!"

I was like, *Oh no, she is going to stop us*. She might be OK with gay people, but she must not like the idea of 18-year-olds going to clubs and not coming back until the next day. She was doing something in the kitchen, and she returned with some silver objects: ham baguettes wrapped in foil for us to take with us. What was going on?! I was completely and utterly lost for words. Chechi's mom knew her son was gay, and she let his boyfriend and me, his new friend, stay at their house. Now she had prepared food for us to take to a gay club! "Enjoy the club and see you tomorrow," she said, handing us the baguettes. "*¡Buenas noches!*" Oh wow, just *wow*!

Up to that point, being gay had been a life-or-death secret for me. Even in the gay chat room, many boys couldn't tell their parents and kept their worries to themselves. There was no way they could say anything about being interested in other boys. And that's how I'd seen things too. Yet here was a world that I'd never imagined where being gay was seen as normal! Maybe I too could have a relationship like this with my parents? I started to hope.

First, I was taken to a gay bar for a drink. While we were walking in, I was so nervous that my heart was pounding and my hands felt cold. I needed a moment to prepare to go inside, but my friends wouldn't wait for me. They just went in like they were going to a cinema. Inside, I saw men in sexy clothes with eyes like hawks, checking out every guy in there, scanning them up and down. I got very uncomfortable, and I turned to my webmaster friend. He is rather a serious and quiet guy, and I didn't know if he would enjoy this type of scene, but he was totally at ease.

"I can relax here," he said. Relax? Everybody was being scrutinized—what could be relaxing about that? More friends soon joined us and I started to feel somewhat OK. It was a world I'd known nothing about: one where everyone was completely free to talk about who they were.

Later, we moved on to a large gay nightclub. Needless to say, I'd gotten used to the scene by then and enjoyed dancing with my friends for the first time! I think I tried my first alcoholic drink there too. I was 18 years old. (In Japan, the drinking age is 20, while in the US it is 21.) There were many gay men who were open and expressive with their desire, and I was completely astonished by their public affection for each other. Until then, I had not seen this many gay men offline. At 6am, all the lights turned on and it was as if the magic spell was undone and everything went back to reality.

On the way back to Chechi's house, I could see the sun rising and the air was slowly getting warmer. Although my friends were all speaking in Spanish, I felt very connected. They spoke a different language; they came from a different country with a different culture; they had a different hair color and bone structure to me—yet these differences did not matter at all. I had found my family; I felt like I finally belonged.

●

Get ready to tell the world who you are

After I graduated from college in Boston I was admitted to the Parsons School of Design in New York. Something that gave me even more courage was the New York City Pride March (aka the "Pride Parade"). LGBTQ+ people and tourists from all over the world visit New York for this parade ... two to four million of them! The parade packed the streets of Manhattan with colorfully dressed crowds supporting LGBTQ+ people. The year I took part, the companies GAP and Apple were also there, which was a huge surprise to me. I learned that the CEO of Apple, Tim Cook, is an openly gay man. Are people still going to deny LGBTQ+ rights while using a product made by a company with a gay CEO?

But most moving of all for me was that Disney took part, with a big sign saying "Celebrating all families" and handing out Mickey Mouse-shaped rainbow-colored stickers. It was so touching to imagine that even my favorite Disney Princesses, Belle and Ariel, were supporting me. *If Disney is promoting LGBTQ+ rights*, I thought, *what am I afraid of?* Even if there are people who do not agree with LGBTQ+ rights, some of their family members must love Disney, or like singing "Let It Go" from *Frozen*.

I'd been so convinced that liking boys was seen as shameful, yet everywhere I looked was a sea of people here to support me. These famous companies had come to cheer on LGBTQ+ people, so there was no need to hide anything. Now I knew that I wasn't worthless and I gained conviction in my worth.

At Parsons, the art school I attended, the head of the Fine Art department was gay, and his husband also taught at the school. The students accepted it as being nothing unusual. Many of the students themselves were unapologetically expressive. There were those with pink and blue hair, who wore black nail varnish, neon green leggings without underwear, nose piercings, tap shoes, and purple stilettos. There was a teacher who wore S&M suspenders too. If anything, I needed to step up my game! There was another guy I thought looked attractive when I joined the school. Later he proclaimed himself a she and started her transition. Some teachers were lesbian. Day by day, little by little, my mind and thinking changed.

I was confronted with the sight of people being true to themselves. *So what's the problem with me wearing makeup or living as openly homosexual?* I thought. I stopped hesitating to tell people that I was homosexual, and I was glad that my life had become so much easier. When I started assisting a makeup artist and hanging out with the team, they would encourage me to go out with makeup on. We would go shopping together and they chose earrings and heels for me. As much as I was uncomfortable exposing myself wearing these items, I was so happy to wear what I actually loved. It was like I was finally becoming the princess I'd wanted to be as a child. When I was walking out of my apartment, my heart was pounding and I looked down so that I would not face anybody in the building. However, the people in the streets would yell at me, "Werq!", "Did you beat your own face?", and "You give me *liiiife!*" I was so proud of myself!

Yet there was still a spiderweb hanging over my head that I couldn't brush away: coming out to my parents. I was terrified that, if I told my parents I was homosexual, they'd be disappointed and I'd never be able to return home. I didn't have the courage to tell them yet.

At the church gay youth group in Boston, I met a Mexican boy who had told his parents he was gay, been abandoned, then come to the US as a refugee. He was a charming guy with the fluff of a moustache just starting to grow. I thought the same could happen to me. But there was the feeling that, *unless I say something, nothing will change*. I felt trapped, and coming out to my parents was the only way for me to be completely free. The desire for freedom eventually won out against the fear of rejection and abandonment.

Let yourself breathe at last

When I moved to New York, I found a partner. He was an insightful musician with the most beautiful heart. We met online and right from the first day, I felt like I had known him for years. We would hang out often and I truly felt love. He and I would often play a Miss Universe question-and-answer game together. We would watch the show and I would pause every time a delegate was asked a question. I would ask him to answer instead; for example, "If you were to describe yourself as a food, what would it be?" He would answer: "I am honey; I am sweet, natural, and everlasting." My heart melted!

I thought that I could proudly introduce him to my parents, and it would be a great opportunity to come out. Back in Japan, I decided to speak to my parents and put my future life on the line with these first words about my true sexuality.

First, I told my mom. I was looking for the perfect time where we could be alone. When I started the conversation, my hands got cold and I was breathing fast. I said, "Next time you come to New York, there's someone I want you to meet. We have been together for about four years now, and actually he's a man."

After I'd waited nervously for my mother's reaction, she said this: "Since you were little, you've said you don't like being with other boys. I had wondered, so that explains everything."

I was completely unaware that during my first year of middle school my mother visited a mental health clinic to find out if I was transgender. The doctor told her, "We can't diagnose him before he's 18." So, it seems she carried that uncertainty with her all the time.

When I came out to my father, he only said, "I see. You do what you want to do, because it is your life." I don't think his expression was either upset or happy. He was just his usual composed self. I didn't know if he knew about me before then, but it was very anticlimactic. My father has always taken the attitude, "It's your life, Kodo, so live it as you want." On occasions when I came to some important turning point in my life, such as moving to the US, I'm sure he worried about me, but he always supported my decisions. When I came out, I truly felt that he wanted me to be happy. I felt blessed to have supportive parents and I know it isn't that easy and won't work that way for everyone—so you must do what feels best for you when it comes to telling your friends and family.

I had now successfully overcome a major life hurdle and found that my parents accepted me as I am. The heavy anchor that had been weighing down my heart was suddenly raised. I'm not kidding. I went warp speed from the Paleolithic to the 30th century. It was like in *The Wizard of Oz* when the world goes from gray to rainbow-colored. My body and soul were as light as a feather and I felt like if I skipped I'd start to fly! I was completely filled with sparkly bubbles of light!

I'd found friends I didn't need to hide anything from and with whom I could laugh and fool about all I wanted. And I had the ultimate allies: parents who accepted me for who I am.

I could be myself and not hide anything. Yet, this wasn't a makeover. At the age of 24, this was the debut of an authentic Kodo Nishimura.

Finally, my life had officially started.

Being true to myself meant freedom.

The Noble Eightfold Path

Wherever you are in the journey of your own life—
whether you are still taking the first steps toward sharing
your true self with other people, or are far along the road
toward living the life you want to be leading—there
are some simple yet very powerful Buddhist teachings
that can help you find your way. These are part of the
Noble Eightfold Path, which offers ways to live and free
ourselves from suffering. These ways of living help us to
overcome desire and self-destructive actions. They are:

- Right views
- Right thoughts
- Right speech
- Right action
- Right livelihood
- Right efforts
- Right mindfulness
- Right meditation

Right views mean seeing things as they are without
prejudice. As you know, I used to feel bad about myself
because of my ethnicity. Then, one day, I found a photo
book of different tribes of the world. There were photos of
children wearing traditional attire from each culture. One
Asian tribe had slim eyes and a chunky body structure,

while a tribe from Africa had longer legs and dark skin. I realized then that it is wrong to label different ethnicities as superior or inferior. We just come from different tribes and ethnic groups, and it is stupid to compare them. Flicking through that book, I was able to find beauty in the diverse characteristics of my fellow human beings.

That is when I felt that I was looking at myself with the right view. Unaffected by what the media says, I was looking at people as all equally valuable examples of humankind. It is something that I also recommend you do too: take a look at the people of the world.

Height, skin color, and facial structure do not define whether you are beautiful or not. Instead, it is how you best express yourself that helps you shine.

One time, I saw a top model wearing a neon purple outfit that did not suit her, and then a mature lady who wasn't a model but who was wearing a coral-color dress that suited her so well. Honestly, I felt that the mature lady looked much more enchanting. So we cannot rely on youth nor the proportion of the body either. Artistic expression is something that gives us all hope and the power to shine!

Right thoughts is making decisions with consideration, free from anger and rage. My mother once told me: "Don't get angry with people who are not capable of doing something." Let me explain. When somebody is not as professional as I expect them to be, I can get angry. However, if everybody were to do their jobs perfectly, the world would be close to perfection. And if somebody is able to do my job as well as I can, I'm easily replaceable. So I came to understand that it is OK that people are imperfect. It is stupid to expect us to be perfect. Of course, I am unable to do many things—as you know!—and I would not want people to assume I can do everything. When I understand this, I am able to approach people with calmness. I end up being more relaxed, and I can achieve what I want in a peaceful manner, without aggravation.

Right speech involves not speaking badly about others, and not lying. I am ashamed to say that I used to spend days creating parody songs that made fun of my friends' small flaws. I would record these and send them to my other friends. Yes, terrible, I know. But when the person I made fun of turned out to be nice later, my face turned red and I regretted my speech.

It is so important to see other people without prejudice, and to speak about others respectfully.

Right action is a collection of good behaviors, such as refraining from killing, stealing, and cheating. Today, if I happen to drop a French fry on the floor, I'll choose to pick it up. I could easily choose to be lazy and let it lie there, but how would that make me feel? When I do things that make me feel that I am a good person, I am able to love myself even more. On the other hand, if I cheat, even if nobody else notices, I know! I am fully aware of pretty much everything that I am doing consciously. So I choose to live in a way that helps me to love who I am.

This is an important lesson for me. Even if I am not confident in how I look or how good I am, I can act in a way that makes me love myself.

Right livelihood is about finding a lifestyle that does not harm people, including yourself. When I was younger, I used to be surrounded by unhappy people who did not treat me with respect. I was constantly upset, and I ended up passing this negativity on to my friends and family as well. Once I got better at respecting myself, finding the courage to say no, and taking action when I needed to, I became happy. Even better, I started to share Buddhist teachings, speaking up for equal rights, and doing makeup for others, all of which made me happier!

Right efforts mean making an effort to maintain a balanced lifestyle. This lesson is very important to me because I am terrible with this. I like to go to sleep early and exercise in the morning. However, I also like to stay up late and work until the early hours of the morning. I like being a perfectionist and the feeling of pushing myself past my limit. However, whenever I do this, the next day I feel so exhausted and unproductive. So I try to maintain a good lifestyle, otherwise I can get sick. I have learned that it is important to maintain the right balance in order to sustain my productivity. Also, by having a harmonious rhythm of life, I can achieve something without being disrupted. It is a continuous battle for me, so I have to keep reminding myself.

Right mindfulness comes from learning life's lessons and being aware of how to live a good life. Things can get crazy and I can easily be affected by what is happening around me. It is very important that I talk to myself. I like to write my thoughts down on paper and reflect on my emotions. When I understand the meaning of my concerns or anger, the agitation goes away. A friend once told me: "Once you learn the lesson from the painful past, the pain goes away." As you know, I used to get very angry at people who humiliated me because of my sexuality. However, I was able to realize that it was coming from their own ignorance. Due to these experiences, I could be stronger and persevere in my path. I can even speak up to protect others. I don't like to be humiliated, but I am happy that I experienced those hardships as they led me to a more meaningful life. This is how I became mindful about what had happened and turned that anger to gratitude.

Right meditation is about meditating properly, which can help us to maintain a good state of heart. Whenever I am facing a big opportunity, I try to meditate beforehand. For example, before the Miss Universe final, where my skills as a makeup artist were in high demand, I would meditate and visualize coming back to the hotel room feeling very content. In these situations, I tell myself that I am grateful for the opportunity, I am grateful that I am able to have achieved my dream, and I am grateful that I am alive. Meditation helps me not only to be grateful for what I have in my life, but to prepare for the future.

Whenever you are mentally present, you are able to perform your best—just as you visualized beforehand.

●

Change takes commitment

At the age of 24, I came back home to Japan for a while to train as a monk, as I've mentioned earlier. I didn't feel that I needed to publicly announce my sexuality to the other novice monks, so I kept quiet about it, somewhat afraid that the others might make fun of me.

During the training, the novices were divided into men and women. I thought: *Are we divided so that there is no temptation from the opposite sex? Well, what about me?* They did not consider my sexuality. The training was, in a word, strict. The only time we got to relax was when bathing, so inside the shared bath everyone would completely let down their mental guard. For me, it was awkward to be bathing with 90 other men. I had nasty flashbacks to my high-school days. One time, just as I was putting on my underpants, one of the other trainee monks approached, a guy who was as noisy as

Write yourself a letter

Sometimes I write a note for my future self, something like: "Welcome back home, you have successfully completed your project and I congratulate you!" When I come back, I am so happy that everything went great—just like I'd written! But you cannot just pray, meditate, and visualize without effort. I believe this exercise will only work if you have put in enough work and yet are still nervous about the outcome. I love the feeling of being welcomed with a letter after a challenging day.

1   Think about something important you have to do.

2   Now write yourself a letter of congratulations— as if you have already achieved it!

3   Leave this note in a place where you will find it later.

4   When you come back and read this note, how does it make you feel? Reflect on the day.

a baby Godzilla. He addressed me suddenly and loudly: "Hey! When I first saw you, I thought you were a fag."

There were other people nearby and of course they were naked too. *Why's he talking about that? And why here and now?* I thought. At that moment, I felt exactly like I did at high school when someone said, "That kid Nishimura. He's a homo, right?"

But, as I considered what to do, I realized that if I lied this time, I would be no different to that high-school kid who had stood frozen before the blackboard. I had to commit to change right in that moment. All those happy scenes rolled by in flashback before me: my Spanish friends, the out-and-proud LGBTQ+ leaders, the rainbow Mickey sticker, and the sea of people at the Pride parade ... they were all on my side, and even if people started humiliating me, there was nothing wrong with me. If I did not change my stance, it would mean that I agreed with the notion of homosexuality being something shameful. I used to be silent to avoid being humiliated at high school, but was I the same person now? If I didn't change, who would? Japan would never change either. It was now or never ... I took a deep breath, held it, and focused my courage. "Yes, I am," I replied.

The bully was stunned. Suddenly, he started asking pushy questions, like, "So does that mean you have anal sex?" I didn't want to answer questions like that; this was sexual harassment regardless of my sexuality.

Then a friend interrupted the conversation, saying: "Kodo works as a makeup artist in New York, doing makeup for Miss Universe. Did you know?"

When the offensive guy heard that, he was even more surprised. Regardless, he shut up. I got dressed into my trainee robes and headed back to the dormitory. But then I heard someone walking up behind me. "Good luck in New York!" the bully said. I thought he was my enemy, but now he was encouraging me? How did this happen?

I realized that by being sure of myself, being brave, and answering honestly, his attitude had changed too. I was so proud that my own conviction had been able to change somebody else's mind. If I had had a dot of doubt or shame in me, it could have been a different story. The key was that not only did I stand up for myself, but I imagined other people suffering in similar situations. Would I stand up for them too? It was definitely easier to include others rather than just thinking of myself. Doing something for others can give us incredible motivation.

Stay true to your path

It is Japanese culture to read micro-expressions and sense the atmosphere, so I was not used to speaking my mind out loud when I moved to the US. At first,

I sulked and assumed people would understand what I meant without me saying anything. But ultimately it was my loss. I learned to verbalize what was on my mind—and that led to a lot of solutions.

If you want to love yourself, you need to draw lines to protect yourself, and there will often be situations when you need to be clear about what you don't like.

When living abroad forced me to share my feelings, I got better at communicating them, rather than just focusing on facts. For example, at work as a makeup artist in LA, the team leader regularly gave me tasks, such as getting groceries or house cleaning, which were completely unconnected to my main role. I said to myself, "I didn't sign up for this," and became increasingly irritated. I felt that my professional skills were being neglected and I became miserable.

However, precisely because I wanted to work with a positive attitude, rather than sulk, I spoke up and said: "I cherish this team, so I need to be honest so as to maintain a healthy and happy environment for all of us. Recently, I have been expected to do additional tasks unrelated to my work and this makes me feel sad and disappointed, because it seems my time and skills are not respected." Notice that I didn't say, "Why do I have to do groceries and house cleaning? I quit!" Instead, I focused on the fact that I cherished the others and I wanted to keep everybody happy, and I also explained how I was feeling—because while the team leader could defend what they had asked me to do, that person couldn't deny how I actually felt about this.

The team leader instantly apologized, and I felt that I had gained respect. This constructive and firm approach continued to increase my value to the team. So make sure that if you wish to complain about something, you emphasize that: "I respect the team, so I have to be honest and happy to do right by the others." And explain how you are feeling, as other people cannot deny this.

Here is another way to communicate a feeling that is hard for you to vocalize. One time, a girlfriend I truly adore invited me out to eat. But she also invited someone I don't get along with. So, I told her honestly: "I adore you, but I feel awkward trying to talk with your friend. If it's just you, though, I'd love to come, because I feel connected to you and can talk sincerely." In her shoes, I'd have thought, *You're a precious friend and I'd be glad I didn't upset you. Thanks for telling me.* I'd be grateful to the other

"A person who judges me for my color or shape is conquered by greed and desire, and does not know my true self."

Udānavarga 22:12

person for honestly sharing their feelings. When you decline offers, make sure that you show respect to others and let them know you care about their own values.

Of course, despite my best efforts, sometimes I still can't get my message across and the relationship can't stay the same. After all, while I wish we could all understand each other, it's impossible to get on well with everyone in the world. I keep reminding myself of that. But when that happens, I convince myself that I am ready to graduate this relationship and move up.

No one wants to talk about things they don't like. And it's particularly true when the other person is important to you. Once you're aware of this, you can begin to state what you dislike in a positive way, and even turn it into an opportunity to gain respect.

Each person will react differently to the same event. It is wrong for us to expect somebody to feel in a specific way.

Things that tend to worry you, or that people sadden you by saying, or that suddenly make you angry and irritated—these are "annoyance triggers." Identify them and try to analyze them. When you understand how each other's triggers work, you might find a way to start addressing and calming those negative emotions.

For example, I used to get upset if I sent a message to somebody and they did not reply quickly. I would feel neglected or that I was considered unimportant, but this was not always the case. People have their own lives, and some value "in person" communication. When I was hanging out with a friend, he did not look at his phone at all; hence, he did not reply to anybody else during the time he was with me. It did not mean that he was ignoring them. So I needed to learn that what is normal for me may not always be normal for other people. My annoyance trigger has become tamed. I just need to see and understand how other people are thinking and living.

Find the "middle way"

As we go out into the world, it is just a part of life to experience some suffering and to meet those who will disagree with us, just like we may disagree with them. We can only stay true to ourselves as best we can, while avoiding extremes or judgments. When trying to find his own path, Siddhartha Gautama spent six years starving himself in the forest. He learned that this extreme regime did not help him to reach enlightenment. He also says that we cannot reach enlightenment by pursuing desire. Thus he says that finding a good balance and living your own way of life is the best path forward.

I explained earlier how I love staying up all night and working on projects until I am literally dizzy, but I know it is not sustainable or healthy to be awake so late. My life rhythm can be a total mess if I continue like this, and I could get sick easily. So I tell myself: *The middle way! Extreme hard work can be self-destructive, so go to sleep and do it tomorrow!* I feel that it is important to go beyond our limits to grow, but there needs to be a balance.

> **When the effort is excessive, we see the excess and not the beauty.**

●

Let's celebrate diversity

We cannot all be the same, so why try to be like anyone else? Let's celebrate ourselves and others for our differences. I think it's fabulous when people strive for diversity, respecting gender, race, religion, age, etc. Having people with different skills makes the whole team more capable and it's a win–win for everyone. Surely that's an ideal model for society?

But, in reality, prejudice and discrimination still lurk under the surface. For example, I often hear men say things like, "She's too opinionated and outspoken for a woman," or "She has twisted men around her little finger." And I hear women talking about men too: "It's because men are simpleminded," or "He has to man up!" They say these things as if it were perfectly normal. But as I'm someone who understands how both men and women feel as well, it makes me upset. Other people tend not to notice, but I come across lots of situations in daily life where I want to say, "Hey, that's prejudice!" Biological sex doesn't define who we are and how we want to live.

Although I identify as being somewhat feminine, I do not have a female body. However, I had a great opportunity to learn about female bodies when I was invited to be a guest at an event called "Let's Talk," hosted by the United Nations Population Fund in Japan. There, I watched movies about menstruation and learned about the process in detail for the first time. Afterward, I asked my friends and family about it and learned that although this is something they experience each month, it is not always easy, so they appreciate understanding and help. I also tried on a pad myself and felt how uncomfortable it can be. I stepped out of my comfort zone and it gave me a whole new perspective about how I can help others, and I feel more useful as a result. I now think I can be a bridge to encourage others to learn about menstruation to eradicate any stigma around it.

Our family register might say I'm male, but I'm very good at makeup and can advise you on how to walk with style in high heels. So, no matter a person's gender, they shouldn't be pigeonholed because other people think they should be "like that." And, whatever someone's gender, we shouldn't force some sort of "you need to be like this" ideal on that individual. Also, nobody should be disrespected by being categorized in a group. For me, a diverse society is one that acknowledges each of our special characteristics, and which appreciates and makes use of everyone's individual story and uniqueness.

In Japan, people say things like, "As a Japanese person, you should know these Chinese characters," or "You have to behave like an adult." But I think these expressions lack consideration. There are Japanese people who grew up in Brazil who do not speak Japanese. There are people who are over 18 years of age, but who were never taught how to read. How would they feel to hear those statements?

We can never expect people to act in particular ways based on their gender, race, or nationality—something that can be easily seen and described. The soul does not have a gender, race, or nationality. Our physical attributes may be similar, but we won't think in the same way. We might assume something like: "You are a transgender woman, so you love men, right?" But being a transgender woman just means that person is a transgender woman, and we can never know who they love just by looking at them.

Just because people who look like you are listening to a certain type of music doesn't mean we all have to dance together.

3

We Are
All Equal

3

We Are
All Equal

● ● ● ● ●

Open your heart and celebrate the fact that
we are all equal and valuable, just as we are.

In Buddhism, there is an important principle called
"dependent co-arising." This is the belief that there is a
reason for everything. Nothing exists on its own; ripple
effects will always occur between things and there
will be chain reactions. So we are caught up in a circle
of cause and effect. It can be a struggle to recognize
our own place in this and to acknowledge our hidden
prejudices, and how these may affect others too.

For example, we tend to blame people for their
actions or opinions. Maybe somebody discriminates

against LGBTQ+ people, but that is not because they want to hate somebody for no reason. Maybe that person did not grow up with other people who are open-minded; maybe they were raised with cultural or religious values that went against LGBTQ+ people; or maybe they are not very happy with themselves so they want to blame somebody else for their misery.

We can hold the person accountable for their opinions—and that is accurate to a point—but we need to think further. What is causing them to resort to hatred, or why do they have a difference of ideas? I think it is very smart to process our reactions this way, and steer away from anger. When we understand the history and context of where everybody comes from, it is easier to cope with people and understand them. As Michelle Obama says, "It's hard to hate up close." So let's focus on the cause and not the effect. If you learn where the ideas are coming from, we can better understand each other. How about I open up and share some stories?

There are some things that I didn't want to share before, things I tried my best to hide, that I want to tell you about now so that we are on an equal footing:

- I come from a privileged household
- I am very judgmental
- I have struggled to talk about my sexual desires

You won't become the real you unless you face up to what you've avoided most.

●

I hid my sexuality and my privilege

I come from a wealthy family, especially compared with the people that I grew up with and spent time with. My family runs the temple and owns properties that we rent out, while my father was a university professor who was paid well, so we never suffered from financial scarcity. I was able to go to a university in the US, and that costs more money. I never had to work part-time or do anything that I did not want to do for money. Because of this, I often experienced jealousy from other people, so I felt that I shouldn't talk about my financial situation openly.

When I was in New York, I knew someone who said that she often used to eat instant noodles to survive, and who worked three jobs to achieve her dreams. And I had a friend who suddenly turned away from me, because I mentioned my visit to Disney World. He said that he worked his butt off and he never had the luxury of visiting Disney World nor eating at fancy restaurants. And then there was an older guy who would criticize my friends and me because our university fees were paid for by our parents, and who said we were slackers. He would talk about his hardships in the past when he had to work tirelessly and ask his friends to feed him.

I suffered from loneliness growing up, and I did not want to become even more isolated because people assumed I had it easier in life. When it came to dressing myself up, I didn't want to outdo anyone else, because I didn't want to be envied by others. I would always find a reason to degrade myself so as to avoid unwanted attention and jealousy and becoming isolated again. I didn't want to appear too perfect, healthy, and happy. I would go to sleep late and ruin my health because I did not want to be radiant. As I became more known and successful through my work, my urge to hide only grew.

I started to ask myself: *How can you grow as a person if you keep trying to downplay yourself?* Then I realized that it was this hiding of my true self, assuming that other people were less fortunate than me, that made some people feel upset with me. During a conversation with a friend, I realized that being transparent is the way to connect with more people. Because I am happy and privileged, I can be a ladder for others to climb and find hope for themselves. There are things I can do because I am no longer hiding my true self.

I have also seen the other side of privilege: my work as a makeup artist put me in a rarefied environment, so I was able to meet extremely wealthy and beautiful people. I met a rich lady who lived in a huge apartment in Manhattan, carpeted with fluffy rugs and flowers everywhere. She had helpers who took care of her, but I sensed that she felt alone and frustrated at being ignored by her children. I also met a stunning model who was in an abusive relationship and would cry while her makeup was applied. I learned that money and beauty really do not equal true happiness.

> Happiness is like wind. You can step outside and find it anywhere—or you can just ignore it, stay inside, and not allow yourself to feel the breeze.

Let go of judgment

I am very judgmental. Are you surprised? I am a masterful flaw-finder. I can tell if every strand of hair is going in the right direction and if your nails are cut neatly; I can spot wrinkles in clothes, and even tell how you are feeling by reading your micro-expressions. I can basically tell if a person's house is clean or not by the way they carry themselves!

This is another thing I wanted to hide about my personality after I became a public figure. I was a horrible person for sure. My favorite things were stormy days because other people seemed to hate them. I was happy when others were unhappy.

When it came to my sexuality and my eczema-prone skin condition, I was definitely in hell for many years, so I hated anybody who was heterosexual and had clear skin. I would feel ugly and chubby, and I hated to look at myself in the mirror or in photos. Because of the shape of my eyes, I never smiled, and if I did try, I would say, "I look so creepy." This anger would make my skin even itchier, and I would scratch my whole body and feel even more miserable and hopeless.

When I was isolated in the classroom, which was almost every day at high school, I would identify something bad about everybody else. I would think to myself: *That guy has a hideous haircut.* Or: *Her makeup is terrible, doesn't she have time to prepare herself to look presentable in the morning?* I would often think, *Nobody is smart here* or *Everybody is so hopeless.* Even when I managed to make a few friends in the US, I would still make fun of them, making those parody songs I mentioned earlier. I would judge people for their

"Whoever strikes finds a man who strikes; the foe finds enmity; the abuser finds the abused; and the angry find the angry."

Udānavarga, 14:3

fashion, physical features, age, education, background, etiquette, you name it—I was excellent at finding the flaws of anybody in a heartbeat. I would even make fun of their detergent smelling too cheap, or if someone was not successful enough.

I could not allow other people to be happy and flourish because I was so angry about my sexuality and how the world did not welcome me. I was a vicious, mean, and hateful person for years. Even today, I can re-live these sentiments sometimes. But if you are able to pin down the flaws of everybody else in a heartbeat, you can also notice gazillions of flaws within yourself. There were countless things that I hated about myself, and I learned that as long as I kept criticizing others, I could never learn to love myself. When I decided to love myself, I learned that hating others would never help me.

What you do to others will reflect right back at you.

I am much, much better today. Now that I think about it, it is when I met people like Chechi and Kami, who accepted me, and when I finally came out to my parents, that things changed.

People would be extinct if not for sexual desire

As you know, for many years I didn't want to show my interest in other men. I didn't want people to think I was creepy or perverted. Even worse, once I became a Buddhist monk, I did not want to share my sexuality with others because of the precepts. But I am only human. Of course I have sexual desires, and today I am determined not to be ashamed of this. I also experience anger, jealousy, and other difficult emotions.

In Japan, monks can get married and have children, but in Thailand they remain celibate. However, if you contain yourself too much, there can be negative consequences. I saw a documentary once about a group of Thai monks who sexually assaulted nuns, and a sexual-health doctor told me that sexual desire is uncontrollable for some people, so it is not healthy to contain it forcefully. On the other hand, I am also very aware that STDs and HIV can be passed on by frequent and unsafe sexual conduct. I feel that some things are good in moderation, just like alcohol. (On that note, friends, please educate yourself about safe sex. Especially PrEP, which is a type of pill that you can take daily or before and after sexual relations, that can prevent HIV infection by 99 per cent. The HIV infection rate is higher among homosexual men, so let's all work in tandem to support the community.)

Anyway, am I a holy person at peace with myself? No way! When I was first featured in the media, it was like I was pretending to be a person who had got his act together; and it felt like imposter syndrome. If you do not allow yourself to feel the way that you feel, you are not living as a complete human being. Why was I alive if I was not being honest with my feelings? To please other people? I felt trapped in a cage because of my identity as a monk.

You can never make people happy unless you are happy yourself.

Then I read the precepts again. It described a lot of anecdotes where the monks were not being respectful to women, spitting on them or taking advantage of them for power. These stories did not necessarily say that sexual desire is bad, but—to simplify it somewhat— that it is bad when driven by bad intentions and bad manners. Also it says that sexual desire is never-ending, so it prevents people from feeling at peace. It can be addictive and cause suffering; I get that!

I realized that there is nothing wrong with such feelings, and Buddhism didn't ban these emotions.

It just says that it is wrong to disrespect others, and sexual desires can distract you from feeling at peace, because you will start to want more. Well, there is a saying I heard from my friend: "The sinner is closer to the teaching, because they can really understand the meaning of the teaching."

When I understood this, I accepted my desire, and now I do not mind talking about my sexuality to others. I am alive and have desires, and there is nothing wrong with that. If I decide to refrain from something, it is not because it is written in the teachings, but because I have learned those lessons myself first-hand; I know I will never learn anything unless I have gone through it. Today, I want to encourage people not to suppress their emotions. It can be so stressful that you may start being mean to others, and you may feel like you are not living.

Anyway, the point here is that I am not naturally a positive person. I was able to grow out of negative situations because I exceeded the limits. I was not able to grow when I hid who I was, or when I hated people to the point of also hating myself, and buried my emotions so deep that I felt like I was not alive anymore. I exploded out of these limitations and ended up being able to appreciate the teachings myself.

When training to become a monk, I came across this astonishing Buddhist precept: "Lying to your heart is a sin." Until recently I lied to myself, subconsciously believing in what society idealized. Today, I no longer desire what everybody else seems to want. I believe it is much better to be in sync with your own heart.

I do not have to be ashamed about feeling good, and I am not afraid to be transparent, because that is how I can inspire others. The truth is that even if you have experienced rock bottom, you can still feel beautiful, healthy, and happy. I am living proof of that!

Discover the Four Noble Truths

There are four beliefs that contain the essence of Buddhist teaching. They are:

The truth of dukkha: the fact that suffering exists in life. As long as we have desire as human beings, there will always be suffering.

The truth of the origin of dukkha: the fact that there are reasons for this suffering. The suffering is ceaseless because of our desires.

The truth of the cessation of dukkha: the fact that if you diminish desires and act right, you will be liberated from the suffering and will reach enlightenment.

The truth of the path leading to the cessation of dukkha: the fact that the way to reach enlightenment is through the Noble Eightfold Path (see page 105).

I used to think that I had to be in a relationship to be happy, and that I did not deserve to be loved unless I was beautiful and confident. I suffered through not having a boyfriend and blamed myself. I strived to be more attractive and confident, but I could never reach how I wanted to be. I thought that I could not be happy.

However, when I started doing makeup for beautiful models, I realized that everybody is human. I learned that beautiful people are not necessarily happy, and beauty and confidence do not always lead to happiness. It is up to me to find happiness for myself. This realization was possible because I was able to go beyond my old ways of thinking. By meeting and talking with new people and going to new places, I was able to start seeing without prejudice and to perceive the truth.

Put aside prejudice

It's truly inaccurate to pigeonhole people and make assumptions about their personalities based on categories. But I admit that I have often done this too.

"Because he's a man."
"Because she's Asian."
"Because they're gay."
"Because she's from there."
"Because he is wealthy."
"Because they're experienced."
"Because he is famous."

When the Iraqi representative attended Miss Universe, I was a little startled and uneasy. I did not know enough about people from Iraq, and I suddenly remembered the religious context and the war. I got a bit scared to meet her.

But she just said, "I've come to this contest to represent people who belong to many religions and cultures in Iraq. There are people who would do anything to achieve peace, and I am their voice. By speaking up, I've received many threatening messages from members of opposition forces. But I have chosen to live my truth. Of course, I don't want to die, but I can't live life lying to myself."

I regretted my wrong assumptions. She was strong-willed, and she empowered me to live my truth sincerely and bravely.

There is no "normal"

After traveling abroad, I had a powerful realization: my suffering was because I'd lived only by the values of the place I'd grown up.

When I was in middle school, a female teacher had an obvious visible panty line. All the students talked about it. But why did it become a topic of conversation? It was because everyone shared an idea of what was "normal," namely, that showing your panty line was embarrassing. The first time I saw women sunbathing topless on the terrace of a Spanish sports gym, I was shocked. *Not just at nudist beaches?!* I thought. When the weather was hot one day, a male friend took off his T-shirt and wore his rucksack on his bare back. It was only me walking next to him who felt embarrassed.

When you realize that your "normal" isn't normal, you become free. If another set of values means it's OK to be seen naked, what's the fuss about a visible panty line? Look at it that way and one of those invisible "it has to be this way" strings tying you down is undone. Don't you feel a little freer? Little by little I dismantled my old attitudes.

If you find yourself in a situation where you think, *That's not normal*, examine yourself before you criticize. When you force your values on someone else, saying, "It has to be like this," you actually shackle yourself with those assumptions and imprison yourself. When you tell someone, "This is normal!", you are forcing yourself to be "normal" too.

> "Normal" is only a measure of your experience; if you know people from around the world, you will know there is no such thing as one type of "normal."

Don't decide your own path according to how others think things should be. And don't force your own opinion as to how things should be on others either. No one needs to walk the same path as you or be forced to change direction, whether that be a family member, lover, or friend.

We all live different lives, and we can never understand what other people are truly thinking or going through. You shouldn't think that you can understand them better than they do themselves, or correct their path for them. For example, for a long time people said I shouldn't wear pink sweaters because I'm a male. But once I did, flowers bloomed in my heart!

Unless you open your heart, you cannot touch another's heart

I believe that unless you understand a thing properly, you've no right to criticize it. I wanted to know Buddhism before I spent my whole life criticizing it, so I became a monk.

Because I grew up in a temple, ever since I was little I'd wondered why people prayed to a doll (the Buddha statue) and asked it to take them to the Pure Land, and where exactly the Pure Land is in this universe from a scientific point of view. I once asked my father, "What's so fun about praying to a wooden statue?" While I was growing up, I never once considered a career as a monk. I did not want to follow in the direction that people expected me to go. In fact, I adored long hair ... so shaving my head was completely out of the question!

All the same, while studying at the Parsons School of Design in New York, I came up with the idea of training as a monk. Once a month, we'd all present and critique our creative work inspired by a particular assignment. This time, I had settled on something inspired by Japan, making art based on origami and my eight years' experience of studying flower arranging. But I had no idea how to produce art that could move people. To be honest, I wasn't satisfied with the results. When I compared my work with the pieces made by

others in that international group of students, I realized that I still couldn't express the true me.

There was a boy in our class from South Korea. He was quiet but his artwork screamed talent. One day he told us, "I'm going to leave school for two years to do military service. When I get back you'll all have graduated, so I'll say bye now."

Later, during our final critique session together, he shared a piece of performance art. He put on a military uniform, shouted in a voice so loud we couldn't have imagined it coming from him, and performed a drill that included standing to attention, running, lying down, and push-ups. He accepted everything: that he was Korean, his sadness at leaving everyone in his school year, and his anxiety. His performance powerfully conveyed that he had made up his mind to do military service. And his pain stabbed my heart. I saw this talented artist standing there in front of me, directly confronting the challenges in his life. I realized that I needed to face my own Buddhist roots … something I'd avoided for so long.

My Korean classmate's performance made me remember something my pianist mother once told me: "If you want to say you hate Mozart, first you have to properly understand Mozart." She added, "Unless you have studied Mozart carefully and can describe exactly what you hate about his music, you can't criticize him."

When you criticize something you have to know about it completely. Otherwise you aren't in a position to criticize.

If you only have a partial knowledge, this can lead to prejudice and discrimination. When I saw my South Korean classmate's readiness to meet his fate, I realized that to truly change, I'd have to face the thing I'd tried the hardest to avoid.

At one point I had fiercely disliked Buddhism and Buddhist priests. *Why do priests chant sutras? How can we be enlightened by saying the name of Amida Buddha? What do the Buddhist teachings mean?* I didn't understand it at all. But if you criticize and reject something based only on fragments of knowledge, then you're a shallow person who just complains. When I realized that I didn't really know about Buddhism, I could see that my old criticisms had been based on ignorance and prejudice.

I was just starting work as a makeup artist in the US, but I thought about returning to my roots and throwing myself into Buddhist training. I imagined myself becoming stronger as a person by knowing Buddhism. And I imagined myself as a disciplined person who'd undergone training as a monk doing something that only I can do on the world stage. I was starting to get excited.

I decided to start my training after graduation. My father said, "If that's what you've decided, then good." And my mother, who also went through the training and is a certified monk, gave me her support too. "If I could do it, so can you. It's good to get the training," she said.

I wanted to properly face and accept something I'd avoided ever since I was little. So, for the first time in a while, I arranged an extended stay in Japan to start my monk's training. In the US, Japanese food is very expensive. Now I'd get to eat it every day! Mmmm!

●

Take a risk to step into the unknown

I'm a makeup artist who loves wearing heels and sparkly earrings. Can I really become a monk? I was going to find out ...

I graduated from the Parsons School of Design and returned to Japan to become a monk. My training took place at Konkai-Komyoji Temple in Kyoto and Zojoji Temple in Tokyo in two-to-three-week bursts, five times over the course of two years. These are two of the most prestigious temples in my school of Buddhism: Jodo

Shu. Each session took place in freezing February or scorching August, and it was tough. In fact, it was hell on earth!

Kyoto winters are bitterly cold, but we cleaned the temple barefoot. My hands became red and numb and my legs were bruised from kneeling all day on the floor. The ceremonial forms of the Pure Land school are precisely determined: the angle of your bow; the height you hold your hands in prayer; even the pitch of your voice. If any trainee gets them slightly wrong, it's back to the beginning. Reciting and repeating the sutras over and over again, my voice got hoarse and I started coughing constantly. Later I found blood in my spit. Our legs would go to sleep and would hurt so much from being seated for hours day after day. If somebody were to fidget, they would yell at us: "Would you chant so rudely at your own parent's funeral?" The training was so severe that many people gave up and left.

My mother had always said that the training was fun. *Surely it can't be that hard?* I thought. But when I did the training myself, teachers would yell, "Run!" at me just because I was walking. I wanted to do some shouting myself ... from Kyoto to my mother in Tokyo: "Hey, is there anything fun at all about this harsh, insane training? Are you kidding me?!"

Every day, we had lots of classes that were three hours long and an hour of recap at night. We had to memorize sutras, teachings, and history. We took lots of exams for each subject and had to pass them all. You know I was terrible at history at school? It was so hard for me to memorize the Chinese characters, dates, and facts. During those classes, I was looking at the clock hand moving second by second—*Gosh, I have two more hours of class left, and then we can have dinner; oh well, I have 14 more days of this class, times four*. It was dreadful, and my breathing consisted of constant sighs.

Toward the end of the training, we learned about Buddhist precepts. During this class, I would not look at the clock and I actually enjoyed learning. Among the things we learned were: "Do not drink alcohol," "Do not adorn your body with decorative items," "Do not listen to music; do not watch dancing," and "Do not sleep on a bed raised off the floor." What?! Did that mean that I would have to wear ear plugs whenever the background music in the shops is playing, and sleep on the floor whenever I stayed in a hotel?

I do makeup! I thought. *And I wear heels and sparkly earrings! These elements are something I've fought to establish in my life. I do not want to give up my hard-earned identity. Do I have to quit being who I am?* As training continued, I worried about whether I was giving a bad name to Buddhist monks and damaging the image of Buddhism.

There was something else, too—the differences between the choreographies performed by men and women in the Pure Land rituals. For example, in one ritual the monk steps over an elephant-shaped incense burner to purify the body with the incense smoke before entering the ceremony hall. Men always step with their left foot and women with their right. But as someone who identifies as both male and female, what should I do? I also worried how to advise people in the same situation as me because people cannot be defined and bound by the terms male and female. Traditionally the teaching is something to be quietly "endowed" from the masters. Questions were not permitted. In this situation, could I really become a monk? I thought hard about it but I still couldn't find an answer.

There was a well-respected master who came to teach us, but once again I was told, "No questions," so after a lot of worrying, I decided to ask the assistant teacher who looked after our everyday welfare about my concerns. He did not have the answer right away, but he told me that he would think about it.

Toward the very end of the session, just as everybody was getting ready to go to bed, and we were lined up to do the day's final roll call, the assistant teacher called my name: "Hey, Nishimura, come over here. The master has agreed to listen to your question."

I was like, *What? Am I allowed to leave the room and go ask him that question of mine? Oh no, now I really have to ask …!*

The highly respected master was waiting for me. My heart was beating frantically. I was completely terrified, but I asked my question anyway: "Some of the choreographies are different depending on somebody's sex. Men step over the incense burner with their left foot, women with their right. And how we use an inked fingerprint as a signature: men use their left thumb and women their right. I have transgender friends and those who do not identify as either male or female, including myself. If they were participating in ceremonies, how should I guide them?"

And this is how the master replied: "The ceremonial choreographies we use were developed after the original teachings. Most important is our founder Hōnen's teaching that 'everybody can be liberated equally,' so the left and right choreographies don't matter in the ceremonies. You can teach others to do whichever they feel comfortable with." *Wow!*

The essence of Buddhist teaching is: "Everybody can be liberated equally."

"Well," I continued, "I like to wear shiny things and to dress up, but according to the precepts, I am not allowed to wear what I like. I was thinking that maybe I should not be a Buddhist monk, being who I am."

He replied: "In Japan, priests often have multiple jobs—some are doctors, others are teachers. And they wear different clothes according to their jobs. They do not wear robes all the time. What is the difference between wearing a watch and something shiny? If a person can spread the teachings and help many others, I don't think there is a problem with wearing shiny things." He concluded, "Buddha and Hōnen would be proud and happy for you to become a Buddhist monk."

How could his answer have been any more logical or clear? The dark clouds hanging over my heart were swept away and I felt a bright breeze enter. At that moment, I knew I could become a monk—proudly and truly!

He told me: "Appearances or the gender division for men and women are not the essence of Buddhist teaching." That easy-to-understand reply completely changed how I thought about Buddhism.

I thought of his words again: "Everyone can be liberated equally." As an LGBTQ+ person, I had suffered alone for years, but that Buddhist teaching helped me. That's why I want to communicate the message that "everyone is equal" to people who are still suffering now.

I grew up in a temple and agonized over being LGBTQ+. I carefully watched the people around me so that I wouldn't get hurt and I asked myself over and over again,

"Why can't I just be who I am and be proud?" While I'd been hating Buddhism for 20 years, Buddhism had been wishing for my happiness for more than 2,000 years.

I am so glad that I was brave enough that day to ask my question. Of my own accord, I decided to act. Thanks to that, I heard an important message that changed my life.

●

Why did I become a monk?

My master said that I could wear shiny things as long as I was able to help people. I immediately remembered my friends who were struggling with their sexualities and religious values. Today, my vocation is not about being one of those monks who follow the traditional activities. My role is to shine, attract attention, and let people of the world know that Buddhism respects all our differences and unique qualities. It says that we are all worthy and we must love ourselves, and do not let others judge us.

You cannot see the truth in the dark. Turn on the light, and the fear might just disappear.

"There is nobody who is not going to be liberated by the teachings of Buddha."

Lotus Sutra, 100

Let's say you sense something moving in the dark. Is it a thief? Or even a ghost? And you get scared. But you turn on the lights and see a plastic bag moving in the draft, and that's not scary at all. Fear often disappears when we understand something's true nature. You have to ask and keep asking for the answers until you are able to fully understand. What I learned from my monk master was completely logical and understandable. When I understood how the system works, I became free.

How to free yourself

If somebody tells you that "things have to be done this way," do you always believe and follow them? You might feel pressured to meet certain expectations. The world has a lot of "conventions" and "supposed to be," but they are not necessarily right. These are the three steps that helped free me to be who I am today:

1. Acquiring information
2. Meeting people
3. Traveling

The first of these steps, "acquiring information," is important because if you believe in something that does not fit with what others say, it can be difficult to speak your truth and argue your position unless you know your subject. Finding reasons, learning facts, and educating yourself with truths can fortify you.

For example, I used to be overwhelmed by the thought that LGBTQ+ people should hide their identities because it was something shameful. When I was growing up, it seemed natural that homosexuals should be hated and discriminated against, and I therefore hid my sexuality. At the same time, I knew that there was nothing wrong with my sexuality, but I was only able to truly believe in my value after obtaining this information.

I studied the history of LGBTQ+ rights through movies, documentaries, and books. I learned how hard people fought for these rights. I also learned about LGBTQ+ history from the 25th century BCE—and its existence since at least the ancient Egyptian, Greek, and Roman periods. Also, many Samurais and some monks were homosexuals. Even homosexual animals exist, and there are some animals who change their sex during the span of a lifetime. I talked to a biologist who told me that diversity brings more possibilities for the species to survive. LGBTQ+ individuals exist because they are beneficial. Anybody who says LGBTQ+ is against nature does not understand this. I also learned about LGBTQ+ leaders who are thriving in the world today, such as Tim Cook, Ricky Martin, Marc Jacobs,

Search for your own answers

When I am troubled by a situation or unsure about something, I write it down, ponder it, and collect the opinions of different people to expand my own thinking. I want to explore and understand the issue for myself, and I want to work out the true nature of things via logical explanations that other people can understand too.

1   Think of an issue that is troubling you. It might be the way somebody is behaving, or why there are particular rules in place, or why you feel the way you do about something.

2   Now research the topic online, watch features on TV and documentaries, listen to podcasts, read articles and books to look for historical facts.

3   Ask people for their opinions. Try to speak to
    somebody who agrees and another person who
    disagrees to get a range of personal viewpoints.
    Direct talk will clarify many things.

4   Go out of your community and see how the topic
    is regarded there. Collect as many ideas as possible.

5   Spend some time reflecting on what you discover.
    Has it changed your thinking in any way?

When I was having doubts about Buddhist precepts,
I sought out one of the original precept books called
Vinaya. In Pure Land Buddhism we only studied the list
of what we cannot do, without any clear explanations.
Going further and reading the stories made me
realize that many of the teachings were simplified and
interpreted for a wider audience, which ended up losing
some of the original intentions.

and RuPaul ... the list goes on and on! Many worldwide companies, such as Microsoft, Disney, and GAP, support diversity and inclusion—but I did not know any of this when I was a high-school student in Tokyo.

The second step, "meeting people," was crucial for me to be free. I met gay professors at college who were excellent at teaching, had welcoming and considerate personalities, and were always well-dressed and deeply respected by many people. They were never made fun of for their sexuality any more or less than the heterosexual faculty members. If they were successful teachers at a prestigious school, are LGBTQ+ people inferior at all? No.

Also, meeting my Spanish friend and his mother taught me that gay kids are not always hated. Tasting that sandwich made by his mother before our night out was telling my palate that I was loved.

And then I met my monk master, who told me that being LGBTQ+ is not a problem. Being told these words in person was profoundly powerful. If I had only read or heard about them, it would have been different.

In the same way, being drowned in the sea of people at the New York Gay Pride Parade was an incredible, life-affirming experience. There were so many people I wasn't able to move! All of them supported and celebrated my sexuality. That was a huge blessing engraved on my heart.

Which takes me to the third step: "Traveling." If I had stayed in Tokyo, I would not have learned about

LGBTQ+ rights, or had those incredible experiences I've shared with you—from that church group in Boston, to meeting my Spanish friends, and dancing at Gay Pride.

It is so important that you visit places and break free of your shell, spread your wings, and broaden your horizons.

I was privileged to be able to visit many countries, yet even if you can't, you can still talk to people who come from different backgrounds in your area. You can talk to people online, watch documentaries and movies, and feel like you are in different places. Knowledge is power.

Please know that there is a whole world out there where what's "normal" to the people around you is not "normal" anymore. You owe it to yourself to discover it.

●

Keep it fresh

Ignorance is considered one of the three poisons in Buddhism. Times change quickly and we start to sense that existing attitudes and teachings aren't enough. We can stop the clocks, but we can't stop time. Our age is characterized by constant progress in every sphere, so we need to keep up with this.

Do you find yourself putting up with rules and things you've assumed are normal or conventional? And are they making you suffer? Take a close look at where they came from. For example, why is drinking in public spaces often prohibited? It is because some people are unable to control themselves and disrupt the community. It does not mean everyone will lose control, but the communal rules cannot distinguish between those who can drink sensibly and who cannot. So drinking itself is not a bad thing, right?

As another example, when I was training as part of a Buddhist community where people lived together, I would consider their communal rules to be like school rules. Not something you obey at home too. For example, during the training, we lived in a temple where there were just male/female public baths. I wished it was like a hotel where everybody had their own individual bathroom, but it does not work that way, so there had to be an easy solution—which ended up excluding me.

If you understand the true reasons those "teachings" came about, you can follow them willingly. But if you can't accept them or you think they don't make sense, you can choose to try to do what is right for you. I think the worst thing is to follow the rules blindly without knowing why they exist, or not stopping to think about them and then risk being fooled, manipulated, or controlled by people in power. Sometimes we need to speak up, and it is the responsibility of both the organizer and you to find solutions. Doing something right and doing the right things are different.

There are cultural environments (realities) that inevitably lead to the creation of rules and conventional values. But those values change with the times, so you need to decide whether you want to keep following them or update your values.

Ask yourself: "What are my ideas based on? Are they hurting me or others?" Maybe those commonplace attitudes originally arose to ensure stability for people, but they might not make sense to you anymore. Examine them, understand them, and if necessary reinterpret them. When you truly understand them, you can make them your foundation to build upon.

The people who live today are not inferior to those who created the rules in the past. We are equally able to think, create changes, and make history.

When new medicines appear, why use the old ones?

As a priest and university professor, my father has a wide knowledge not only of our school but of Buddhism across the world and centuries. And there's something my father told me that I strongly agree with.

"Of course priests need to change with the times," he said. "Take doctors. When new and more effective medicines are developed, they use those new ones instead of the old ones. Otherwise, they wouldn't be practicing modern medicine that works better. Society is the same. Now that information is everywhere, we can't ignore it and live as we did in the past. You know, unless priests adopt new teachings and ideas to match the times, we can't help anyone who is alive today."

Are you still relying on old medicine even in these new times? If you have doubts about a medicine's effectiveness, it's OK to change it!

There's a saying in Japan: "The nail that stands up gets hammered down." Sometimes I feel the pressure to conform. But we live in a globalizing world with increasingly diverse values. I think the concept of conformity is "old medicine" in many situations. Much of what we were once told does not function anymore. For example, people might have once come to temples to pray for rain for the crops, but irrigation and fertilizer have since been developed. When you decide to start living a life of self-love, you might find yourself held back by people who believe in conformity. But I want you to keep believing in yourself. Everyone is different, and nobody can tell you who you are, or what you are capable of.

> ## No one knows the future, but who you believe yourself to be will determine your life.

Ideas based on old medicine won't necessarily bring happiness to all people. Everyone has different stories, and I want to have fun making mistakes. Don't give up on your life because of the values of people you don't admire. Try that new medicine and be adventurous. Do that, and I think you'll be truly satisfied with your life.

Failure, people say, is not really failure. Actual failure is the inability to believe in yourself, and giving up.

●

Command respect

You don't need anyone to teach you how to be equal or give you permission to be equal. Being treated as equal has nothing to do with your abilities or what kind of person you are. It is not up to anybody to judge whether you are equal or not. It is not their choice. We are all equally valuable—and that is a fact.

It's about whether you are treated as equal or not that we need to work on. But even before you think about these things, you are already equal to others. The Buddhist saying "everybody can be liberated equally" is an important reminder of this. So let's be brave together. There's no need to feel ashamed or think you're selfish if you recognize that you are as valuable as everyone else.

As a monk and an LGBTQ+ person, when I tell people, "We are all equal," I get a variety of reactions. But one in particular made me happy. It was from a boy in Brazil. "In my religion homosexuality is not welcomed and my mother wouldn't accept that I'm gay," he wrote. "But thanks to what you said, I spoke with my mother and she understood."

In Los Angeles I shared a room with an Italian–American man. One day, he told me: "Since I was little, I've gone to church every week and heard that being gay is a sin. I feel guilty for giving in to temptation and dating a man."

As you know, I have absolutely no intention of proposing that anybody convert to Buddhism, or of criticizing the beliefs of other religions in any way. It's just that Buddhism offers some helpful life advice, so

I told him this: "When I studied Buddhism, I learned that everybody can be equally liberated regardless of their characteristics—so your sexuality does not matter at all. I learned to celebrate who I am and that made my life much easier. I'd like you to know about the existence of that teaching. And on a personal level, I want you to be happy and free of guilt." He thanked me, and it did seem like his stiff shoulders relaxed a little.

"All the names that exist in the world, they merely mean different letters."

Sutta Nipāta, 648

Siddhartha Gautama said that we are all equal, the only difference is in the name. In Buddhism, we are all equal—regardless of gender, sexual orientation, ethnicity, race, disability, occupation, title, education, wealth, or any other types of differences.

Question it, even if it is a pillar of teaching

We don't need to all be the same. And others don't need to accept our values. I want to say something loud and clear: Your beliefs are not the only correct ones! As an example, let's think about Buddhist enlightenment. Generally, people say that the purpose of Buddhist training is to achieve enlightenment. That is why people chant and meditate as though there is an end goal. But actually one academic view says that enlightenment doesn't exist. This is something that contradicts what my school, Pure Land Buddhism, teaches.

When I asked my father, he said that there are many explanations of enlightenment. However, he also said that there is no early Pali sutra in which Buddha explains the nature of enlightenment. In his works on Siddhartha Gautama, the famous scholar of Buddhism, Hajime Nakamura, writes that the Pali sutra references to the Buddha's enlightenment were later additions. (I love how my father is knowledgeable and teaches me about contradictory studies too.)

What the Buddha truly emphasized was the instruction to live rightly (see page 105). He adapted what he taught to the needs of each person. So, when those people transmitted his teachings, they left behind various different interpretations of enlightenment.

Of course it's a wonderful thing when your beliefs —religious or otherwise—provide comfort. But I think it's also important to take a good look at the facts and be flexible enough to accept different ways of thinking, and to examine your own thoughts and emotions too.

●

Meditate on your emotions

Happiness, guilt, anger, sadness—our emotions change constantly everyday in response to the world. That's natural. But it's important not to ignore the emotions that trouble our hearts. We need to find out why they happen, and I believe meditation is a good way to do that. By meditating, we can focus on what is happening in our mind, and that can lead us to a realization.

The traditional form of Buddhism believed only the monks were able to reach enlightenment. However, Buddhism arrived in Japan in the 6th century CE from Korea via China, and in China an adapted version of Buddhism had flourished; now, the teachings are made available to a wider audience, and it was said that everyone could be enlightened by meditating.

There are many ways to meditate in Buddhism. For example, there is *zazen* (sitting meditation with your legs crossed) and *shakyo* (writing sutras). I mentioned earlier how in my school, we chant the name of Amida Buddha, aka Limitless Light Buddha. We repeat: "*Nam Amida Bu*," which means "I devote myself to Amida Buddha." The "*nam*" part is equivalent to Namaste in Hindi, which means "I devote myself to you." We do this because in a sutra, Buddha says: "If somebody chants my name with faith, they shall be guided to the Pure Land by Amida Buddha."

So during my training to be a monk, we'd kneel and chant for hours and hours. Honestly, when I first started chanting, my mind went all over the place. I thought, *How long do I have to chant?* and *What are we doing this for? My legs are already so painful but I have to practice this hour-long ceremony five times a day. How many more days will I have to do this?* I was bewildered, but eventually my mind reached a peaceful and grateful place.

I was able to let go of unnecessary excitement, anger, confusion, and instead feel balanced after contemplating so much. Without the chanting meditation during my training, I'd probably have continued complaining and getting irritated. Meditation helped me feel grateful, and that's what got me through the tough training. Now I meditate on my own to feel balanced, and stop when I feel grateful—and that is enough. Whatever the meditation method is, I think the purpose of meditation is to let go of all the emotions, and find a balance in the heart.

"When you do something, and you regret and experience a bitter outcome, that is not a good action. If you do something, and you are filled with joy without regret, that is a good action."

Dhammapada, 67–68

Meditate to connect to your awareness

This meditation will help you to connect to a deeper level of awareness. The body has a gender, size, and color, and engages in human interactions with the outer world, but I think that the being who sits in the cockpit of our bodies does not have a form or color. It is something like a ball of light. When I get stuck in my life, I try to take away all the other elements, focus on my inner awareness, and have a conversation with myself. I do this by asking myself questions during my meditation.

1   Find a place where you can be alone. It can be in the bathtub or on a beach at night, or you can take a walk somewhere quiet. Turn off all cell phones and any other disturbances. If you are indoors, turn off all the lights and sit on the floor.

2   In order to focus on your awareness, it is helpful to stare at another light source. It is easier to

concentrate your gaze outwardly on this while focusing your attention inwardly on your emotions. It could be a candle flame or even the moon. I prefer a natural light source and not LED lights. You can also sit in total darkness.

3   Ask yourself the following questions if you feel overwhelmed and want to balance your emotions:

- Do I choose to be affected by this situation?
- Am I stronger than what is causing me trouble?
- Why is this happening?
- What will be the consequence if I do not make changes now?
- Why am I subconsciously choosing to feel this way?

This can help you reconfirm what makes you sad and what makes you angry, as well as the reasons for this. You can look at your situation objectively and order your mind.

4   Ask yourself these questions any time you wish:

- What do I really want to do in this life?
- Is this life a reality?
- What if life is just an illusion?
- Is there something that I haven't done in my life that I must do?

- What should I do to ensure I have no regrets when I die?
- Why am I living the way I am today?
- If I could make all my dreams come true, what would I want?
- Why am I alive?
- What makes me happy?

Of course there are no easy answers, but I am constantly thinking about these things. As a result I am less affected by society and my circumstances. After all, your life is yours and you can only experience your life in your body. You are free to make your own decisions and take control. Do not let anybody take advantage of your existence.

5   Stop when you feel it is enough, and come back when you need to.

6   If you want to write down your thoughts, this will help you to remember the takeaway insights that apply to your daily life.

Meditation creates a precious opportunity to withdraw from your body, which is a container, and to see yourself from the perspective of the universe.

"Balance yourself, and guide others. If you do that, wise man, you will not suffer."

Dhammapada, 158

●

Prayer

Meditation is for balancing your feelings and connecting with your awareness. On the other hand, prayer is for wishing for things over which you have no control. You could call prayer a form of "consolation," and that's not untrue. But don't you think prayer sometimes makes things easier and calms our minds?

My constant prayer is: "May I retain a sense of gratitude and a positive mind." I don't pray for things that hinge on me working hard. The way I see it, prayer is a kind of lucky charm to provide peace of mind when you've already done everything else or you have no control over the situation.

Be the change you want to see in the world

Of course, being part of a minority involves a little extra work, a lack of freedom, and what you might call difficulties. Despite that, I'm proud to be who I am. People often say to me, "LGBTQ+ people still aren't accepted in Japan; the government doesn't change, people are hard-headed and Japan remains so far behind." That is true to a certain extent. Yes, I did see male couples walking down the street holding hands in the US and Spain, and I have not seen that happening in Japan except for in Shinjuku Nichome, an area of Tokyo with many gay bars. But in pretty much every country or culture there are some people who can come out and say they are LGBTQ+ and some who can't.

Your culture may affect how easy or hard it is to declare publicly that you are different from others, but ultimately it depends on whether or not you have the conviction to be proud of yourself. You can't blame where you are. When you think you can't live your truth in your current environment, you make it extra hard for yourself. When you just talk negatively, you will begin to think the situation can never change. I realized that being negative would limit my potential and I would be left feeling incapable. To me, being positive and optimistic is the only way to sustainably improve the situation while maintaining my own mood. Otherwise you will start to hate everybody, and if you hate people, you will hate yourself as well eventually. That's why it's so important to look on the bright side, find positive interpretations, and be creative.

And not just for LGBTQ+ issues either. Some people call their own society and culture "no good" or backward. But I still think it's important to be intrepid and make changes. If I change, other people will change too. I could avoid change and leave it up to the rest of society. But then I wouldn't be my true self. I want to change, not just for myself but for those experiencing the same pain. It can be scary, but if you stand up for yourself and all people who are similar to you, as well as those in the next generation, you will have more reasons and meaning behind what you say. Do it for yourself; do it for others; do it for the future.

●

Acknowledge that life is interdependent

Buddhism says that everything is related. Everything consists of other elements, and nothing is truly independent. If we help one of us, we help everyone.

When I was younger, I used to compare myself to others and think, *I want to be the first in line*, or *I want to have more things than others.* However, the universe is connected. Therefore if I give more happiness to the people surrounding me, I receive more happiness back.

There are some people who appear to want to dominate the world's wealth, yet I think sharing wealth brings even more happiness to ourselves. It is great to attain it and share it. I respect Drew Barrymore because she shares what she has, and inspires us to work for others out of kindness and compassion. I love when she shows examples of other inspiring people who she calls "Drew-Gooders" on her TV show. In 2007, Drew was named the Ambassador Against Hunger for the United Nations World Food Programme (WFP) and visited a camp in Kenya. I was curious about why a well-known actress would want to give back to less fortunate people than herself. At that time, I thought, *If I was well-known and wealthy I would spend my money just for my own benefit.* She made me reconsider. What I came to understand is that learning about the situation of the world helps you understand how privileged you are, how you can share happiness with others, and that the smiles and gratitude are multiplied when they are returned to you. That is why I decided to try to give back to my community and inspire people.

Doing LGBTQ+-friendly makeup seminars and sharing makeup tips with people of all genders, especially transgender women, has been very fulfilling. I introduced techniques such as how to cover a five o'clock shadow using orange concealer. (The bluish shade can be counteracted with the opposite shade of orange.) When I see the happiness on their faces, and hear them say, "I used to not want people to look at me, but now I can finally look up and say, 'Look at me!' I feel like Cinderella and I strutted the street," I feel like this is why I learned the art of makeup!

I have also created a rainbow sticker in collaboration with the Japan Buddhist Federation. I made the sticker with the palms together in the middle and a rainbow in the background. I think this will encourage people to learn about the teachings of Buddhism that support diversity. Not only the lay people but also those who work in temples can deepen their knowledge in this way. These stickers can be placed at the entrance of temples to show support for all people without discrimination. People have been sending me messages about how empowered they have felt seeing them, and how the message of Buddhism can even save people through graphic designs such as this sticker.

The joy I experience back is doubled because life is interdependent—so if I can consider myself as beautiful, we make the world more beautiful too. And that is what we are going to be looking at next.

4

Fall in Love with the Beauty of You

4

Fall in Love
with the Beauty of You

● ● ● ● ●

*You have a special beauty that only you can
bring to the world. Let your true colors shine.*

As you might have guessed by now, I'm a huge believer
in the power of makeup and fashion. Of course, we all
know what's inside is important, but your appearance is
the topmost layer of you, and people can see that.

People tend to think of Buddhists as being simply
dressed, but actually some teachings put extreme
emphasis on appearance. For example, there is a
Mahayana Buddhist text known as the "Flower
Garland Sutra," which refers to a special figure called
Guan Yin and states the following:

"They will not listen to one in shabby clothes.
Sublime virtue requires sublime appearance."

This teaching is an exhortation to adorn our bodies.
The sutra also says:

"The Bodhisattva had many followers of
handsome and majestic body who, according to
the teaching, wore beautiful ornaments, and who
were wise and excellent in knowledge."

And:

"The Bodhisattva is said to have had a beautifully
ornamented appearance and taught the people
while wearing the most pristine clothes, while
wreathed in the fragrance of many kinds of flower
and with a garland of flowers on his head."

Be inspired by the example of Guan Yin

Guan Yin is a Bodhisattva, someone who is soon to be
a Buddha. Next time you happen to see an image of the
Guan Yin, please look closely. Most of the images are
depicted with a golden crown, necklaces and earrings,
and their outfit is made up of layers of delicate fabric.

The almost royal outfit Guan Yin wears is associated with the original Buddha, Siddhartha Gautama, who was a prince before becoming a monk. Guan Yin was introduced in Buddhist sutras during the 1st century BCE, and was originally thought to be a male hero in India. However, Guan Yin was later described as Goddess of Mercy and Compassion in China. There is a saying associated with Guan Yin: "If you want to be a Bodhisattva like me, you should dress up lavishly, be wise and strong, so that people will respect you. That way, you can give guidance and save more people." This approach was the opposite of what I had learned in the beginning! I thought Buddhism only valued a humble outlook. The name "Guan Yin" signifies somebody who can see sound, which means being able to hear the voices of people suffering. Guan Yin empathizes with them and saves the world. How inspiring!

I have personally been encouraged by the example of this gender-ambiguous figure, who dresses so lavishly.

Who'd have thought a Buddhist teaching would tell us to be fierce, fabulous, and flawless?

Your appearance can reflect the inner you and become a representation of who you truly are. When you need to stand up and speak up, if you wish to be respected by others, your appearance can help. And it's important that you are able to respect yourself too. This will act as a megaphone to amplify your presence.

When I worked on Miss Universe, the contestants were already so beautiful that I wondered if they were also human beings. But in preparation for the competition they paid attention to every strand of hair, applied their makeup perfectly, and put on clothes that made them look even better, transforming them into women so beautiful that everyone gasped with astonishment.

I think it is not healthy to value people based on their facial features or physical structures that cannot be changed, because essentially you are judging other people, which will reflect back to you. You will end up being unable to embrace yourself. However, wearing something that fits you, and learning how to do makeup and hair to compliment your features, will make you feel empowered. Our appearance can give enormous power to the inner beings!

I have lots of fun dressing up. But I don't do it for anyone else. I do it to love myself. After all, I think we should be respected for our hearts.

I wear makeup and heels not only to demonstrate who I am, but to show that there can be somebody like me. There must be people out there who want to try wearing makeup and high heels but fear what others think. I want them and the world to see me and realize that it is OK for a male to wear makeup and heels, and walk like nobody's business—which, by the way, I can!

When I was little I never saw anyone like me in Japan. I was made to believe that being the real me was wrong. I pray that people will see me now and think, *It's OK to be who I am.*

●

Study your style

I'm sure many people know that their appearance is important, but don't know what suits them, or how to improve their fashion sense. In fact, I once had no idea how to brush up my appearance either. I thought I was pretty stylish. But when I see some of my old outfits in photographs, I often want to use a time machine to prevent them from ever happening!

A method that works well for me is to make a "Worst of Me" album with photos of myself when I did not look good. I use it to mercilessly reassess what suits me and what doesn't. (Of course, the album is visible to me and me alone!) I am so regretful about these images, but these are the steps that were inevitable for me to grow.

Make your own "Worst of Me" and "Best of Me" albums

If you scream with regret at the old you, why not make a "Worst of Me" album of horrible old photos to refine your style and help you learn what not to do?

1   Go through your old photographs on social media and elsewhere on your laptop or phone.

2   Select the images that you know don't show you at your best, especially the ones that make you cringe!

3   Also find photos that you love, and study why you like them. (I am just talking about your makeup, hair, outfit, and posture here.)

4   Consult the photos whenever you are about to buy a new item of clothing or styling yourself.

5   Share your albums with friends you trust. When my friends saw my "Worst of Me" album, they were blunt and harsh but also gave me plenty

of valuable advice: "Keep your hair short, wear something inspired by traditional Asian outfits, don't pose too exaggerated, smile big even though your eyes disappear ..." It was so detailed! Some advice I took; some I let go.

At Parsons, there was a girl who wore tap shoes that looked so stylish. I asked if we could shop together and she gave me lots of advice. I accepted help from other people and perfected the styles that suit me.

Don't chase after fake beauty by trying to be someone else. Find your own beauty, then nobody can beat your original style.

By looking at the "Best of Me" album I realized that turtleneck shirts made my neck look neat and tidy and sleeveless shirts emphasized my vertical lines and made me look taller! I looked at clothes I'd worn and noticed lots of things that suited me. My friends would tell me, "That kind of exotic Asian look suits you, Kodo. Why don't you try a more elaborate style? Try something not many people wear." I thought, *They are pushing me to be the person I want to be*, and tried it out. Again and again,

I found styles that worked and my closet started to fill with clothes that suited me.

Once, I wouldn't think twice about going out in only a flappy vest top and walking around town with my stained, shabby rucksack. I'd catch sight of some sad unfortunate soul, then realize I was looking at myself in a mirror and get a huge shock. But once I started wearing clothes that suited me, I glimpsed myself in shop windows and I looked great! It was wonderful. And I'm so happy that even though my build doesn't change, different clothes can create such different impressions.

I still take photos of myself, assess whether clothes suit me or not, and check the balance of my whole body. This process is tedious yet it makes a world of difference! When my clothes suit me really well, they look like they were made for me, and now I've found a personal style that represents me authentically.

Keep giving yourself compliments as you transform and if you see someone looking nice, compliment them as much as possible too. I think it is wonderful when it works both ways, and everyone gets to be more stylish.

It's makeover magic! Compliment and be complimented—and create a synergistic effect.

I thought that V-neck shirts were sexier, but they made my neck look too long. I thought wide, short pants were cute, but they made my legs look short. In photos I opened my eyes wide to make them look bigger, but this created wrinkles on my forehead. I had foundation that photographed grayish in pictures, too thin brows, too much contouring—the mistakes were endless!

Hairstyle, eyebrow shape, gestures ... they were all failed attempts to be someone else. I looked hard at pictures of me that I'd rather not see, and repeatedly screamed, "Nooo!" I saw that those styles hadn't suited me, and that was the first step to developing a more sophisticated eye.

Once you understand your awful mistakes, you'll never make them again. It's the same with the Buddhist precepts; you cannot fully understand anything unless it is a learning you acquired first-hand. If something doesn't make you look good? Get rid of it or recycle it. If clothes don't suit you? Don't buy them again. If hairstyles and makeup doesn't suit you? Sayonara forever!

Shaving my head

Just before I left the US for Japan to train as a monk, my makeup artist boss shaved my head. I'd always dreamed of long silky hair and back then I used to get my hair chemically straightened. So I was more than a little reluctant to shave it off. But my boss had planned a surprise birthday party for me to take place right after I got my monk's haircut. My boss even drew my lips with black eyeliner and put crystals on my head. I was looking like a bedazzled goth fashionista. Friends were complimentary, saying that the look suited me and that I had a beautifully shaped head. Because of the amount of compliments I received, I gave in. I admitted that I look good with shaved hair. I began to feel confident about my short haircut.

As you know, I used to have a complex about my almond-shaped eyes, but the elder sister of my Spanish friend Chechi once looked straight into my eyes. "Kodo, your eyes are beautiful!" she said. It was nice to be complimented, but I didn't believe her straightaway. "What are you talking about?" I replied. "Your blue eyes are far more beautiful!"

A famous photographer who takes photos of Miss Universe said this too, adding, "Your eye shape is nice, though a little eyeliner wouldn't hurt." Getting compliments like that gradually changed my thinking. Still, I didn't suddenly start to love my eyes. Being complimented was only the first step toward accepting them. I studied smoky eye makeup to highlight the particular character of my eyes and looked for

"Jealous, stingy, lying
people, even if they have
a beautiful exterior, are
not elegant.

A person without these,
who can eradicate anger,
is a wise person—they are
called elegant."

Dhammapada, 262

eyeshadow application to suit my own style and, in the process, gradually came to love these eyes of mine.

I dare say I could use various techniques to make my eyes look bigger. But as soon as you start trying to be something you aren't, that's imitation and being fake. It might feel nice for a second, but the moment I see that it is fake, the illusion is lost. Study what's special about you, because makeup that brings out those features will make you shine. My own eyes taught me that.

I've tried using glue to make a double eyelid; I also tried pushing the bone above my eyes with my fingers during yoga so that the bone would indent and make them appear bigger. They were brave efforts but nothing happened. My eyes may not be the ideal ones I pictured, but I later found people who have even thinner eyes than mine who looked beautiful. It is not about the fold, but if I choose to love my eyes or not. I was not really being kind to myself.

It is a choice to love and accept yourself.

When I was starting out, I used to experiment with my makeup from evening until the following morning. The whole night long! Even though it made me dizzy the next day, this experience really improved my makeup skills. You have to exceed a limit to go somewhere new in my opinion.

If you put on the same makeup every day, you'll never find a new look. Once in a while, try spending hours on your makeup, doing it slowly and carefully, reapplying until perfection. Take photos, adjust, and study the features of your face, how it moves, and find your best look. I'm sure you'll notice an improvement!

Makeup is somewhat like cooking. Try different recipes, add more salt, cook longer, add spices. Try to find what works for your face.

It is not just about you, but what surrounds you too

Personal possessions and accessories create a full picture. They form part of that person's aura. Bags, slippers, socks, your pen, the chair you sit in, even the plastic bottle you drink from. When you consider that these are part of you, you start to choose your personal items with care. There's absolutely no need for them to be expensive. The way to decide is whether it aligns with what you are trying to convey.

During the Miss Universe competition in 2018, I worked as a makeup artist. I offered a glass water bottle to Miss Universe Philippines, Catriona Gray, and she told me she didn't want to be seen carrying it! That's how much attention to detail is involved. I was shocked. But I believe that much consideration is required for promising results. Catriona Gray won the competition and was crowned Miss Universe 2018! No wonder.

If you really want to express yourself beautifully, you need to focus on your personal items as well as your inside and outside.

My guess is that many people are scared of standing out, so play it safe with makeup and fashion. I was once afraid to go out wearing makeup because I didn't want others to find out I was a male who used cosmetics. It took courage whenever I went out wearing high heels.

At the Miss Universe pageant, the contestants wear 15cm (6in) heels and walk in a fierce way to highlight their long legs. They look so elegant and full of confidence! I wanted to wear heels too but I was nervous about being laughed at. When I was in Japan, I wore platform sneakers with three insoles stacked inside. Later, during the Pride parade, I saw people who were naked apart from being body-painted in rainbows. After seeing that, everything was OK for me. Again, mind-blowing and life-changing! So I hit the shoe store in West Village and I noticed that black wedges in heels that cover the top of the foot are quite gender-neutral. I started wearing them and I felt like

Cinderella who'd regained her glass slipper! Later, I collected many types of high heels.

●

Eyeliner and mascara can change your life!

The Princess Diaries is one of my favorite movies. Julie Andrews plays the queen of an imaginary European country who suddenly appears in the life of a boring (frankly, rather dorky) American high-school girl played by Anne Hathaway. She teaches this girl the etiquette and refinement she needs to be a princess. It's a story about a girl with shaggy hair and eyebrows being completely transformed by the power of hair-styling and makeup! Of course, since she's a Hollywood actress, she turns into a beguiling beauty. It's astonishing.

At the film's climax, the girl gets soaked in the rain but shares her feelings in her own words. The final scene where she gives a sincere speech and everyone applauds is so moving. The story shows that a new outside can change your inside too. Once you gain the confidence, you do not need makeup anymore. It made me realize the importance of how our appearance can change the way we see ourselves.

I mentioned earlier how it was a book about Miss Universe Japan that first got me interested in makeup.

When I read that "the dark pupils of Asian people can be brought out with eyeliner and mascara," I thought, *If Miss Universe is doing it, I must too!* So I went to a Boston drugstore and bought my first ever eyeliner and mascara. When I tried the mascara out and saw the effect on my lashes, I thought, *What's going on? How much longer will they get!* I was moved and delighted. There was a powerful feeling that my life would soon change. When I was in Japan, at the cosmetic counter of a department store, the female clerk would often ask me, "Are you looking for a gift for your mother or girlfriend?" and I could not say it was for me. I knew I would be stared at and made to feel unwelcome. But in Boston, there were male clerks wearing perfect foundation and glitter who were selling makeup. I felt that right here, I might be OK to try makeup.

The first person I ever did makeup for (other than myself) was my roommate, Eri. Her makeup routine was to dab on blue shimmery eyeshadow using the free applicator, and without looking in the mirror. (She was that kind of girl back then!) I couldn't let it go and one day asked her, "Would you like me to do your makeup for you?" When we tried, she looked so different that we could hardly believe it was her face. There was definitely a moment when she realized that she could look prettier than she'd ever imagined. It was incredible how two simple makeup items could give someone confidence.

If I can learn to use foundation, eyeshadow, and lipstick, I can help other people with makeup too, I thought. I had found my mission: to learn the art of makeup and support even more people who accept me for who I am.

●

Discover the "art of getting ready"

I learned this phrase from a workshop given by a makeup artist who worked with Beyoncé, Sir John: "the art of getting ready." Carefully preparing your appearance is an art, just like the Japanese tea ceremony: the process itself is important, not just the end result. And that principle applies to the rest of life too, not just makeup.

During the preparations for the international Miss Universe pageant, the National Director for Miss Universe Japan and I had to style Miss Japan. We planned the styling before the events and appearances, so that it would be easier to coordinate everything perfectly in a short amount of time during the competition itself.

This sort of preparation can be very helpful. Before a special occasion you can consider everything beforehand: the style, if it will suit the venue's ambiance, who you will meet, how long you'll be out, makeup, clothes, shoes, and nails. It's helpful to do a test run, take photos like a look book, and check all is OK.

Try this approach yourself. Even if only once, plan ahead and have a go at doing everything you possibly can to look stylish. Somehow that experience will open your eyes, even when you're not particularly trying hard later on.

Go for your dream!

In my third year at university, I had to do an internship. And if I had to intern, surely I should do something I liked! When I learned about the makeup artist for Miss Universe, I immediately knew I had to intern with her.

I was incredibly nervous but I sent an email to say I'd like to learn makeup, and a reply came right back.

First, she asked me, "Are you competing for Miss Universe Japan?"

I was like, "No, I'm a male! I cannot compete. I just want to learn how to do makeup for a guy."

Later, she said she would charge $1,000 per four-hour lesson! (At this point, please imagine a few pages of exclamation marks.) That was about the same amount as the rent when I'd shared that place with Eri! I thought it was out of the question, but my mother gave me a push.

"You'd be investing in something you wanted to do for a long time," she said. *Wow, my mom said yes ... I guess I have to respond and schedule the lesson?* I made the decision to do it, and it changed my destiny.

When the time comes, don't be stingy! If the matter is important, it's vital to invest in yourself.

Unfortunately, the makeup artist had to postpone our makeup lessons. But to apologize she invited me to a meal and I told her about my enthusiasm for makeup artistry. Then, can you believe what she said? "You and I have the same passion for makeup. I want you to be my assistant!" A decision to invest in my dream had come back as a priceless opportunity. I am who I am because of that decision when the moment came.

Later, I joined the team and slowly started to learn about makeup etiquette and techniques. I started buying makeup products that my mentor recommended as much as I could, and started practicing on my friends from school. At Parsons, there was a photography department, so I went to their shoots and did makeup for their models every week for about three semesters. I was given over ten models per day. I was pushed and rushed, and asked to do more than I physically could. I was told to do various types of makeup—from natural to colorful, to anime, and horror. If I'm honest, I really didn't like to do makeup that made anybody look creepy, yet I truly appreciated the hardcore training I got. I was practicing hard so that I was able to achieve my dream and join the makeup team for Miss Universe.

I used to write in my notebook "I was able to go to Miss Universe as a makeup artist" over and over again, and read this aloud. That would be the only way for me to participate in the competition as a physically male person. Then, the following year, I was able to join the Miss USA and Miss Universe team! It was surreal and I would sometimes feel so scared that something might happen and my dream would collapse before my eyes. During the show, I felt overwhelmed and over the moon. As a makeup assistant, my job included laying out the makeup products, handing makeup products to my boss, preparing the models with moisturizer, and sometimes applying foundation and fixing minor areas. After each day, I would bring the makeup brushes, wash and dry each one, and bring them back the next morning.

I learned so many detailed techniques. For example, my boss told me that mascara isn't good if you apply it too much. It can look gunky, tacky, and unsophisticated. When I was told to remove Miss USA's mascara lumps,

"The scent of a flower
does not go against wind.
However, the scent of
people with good virtue will
defy wind; it will spread in
all directions."

Dhammapada 54

How to apply makeup to bring symmetry to your face

It may sound bad for your face's left and right sides to be different, but it's natural in the same way as the lines are different on your left and right palms, so don't worry! The bone will not move easily, so once you know how to balance your face with makeup, your work is done!

1. If you're struggling to see the shape of your own lips and eyebrows and do your own symmetrical makeup, a good idea is to try taking a photo of yourself and then flip it into a mirror image, from left to right.

2. Have a go now at taking a selfie with your smartphone, then turning it upside down and reversing it from left to right. You can notice many things just by slightly shifting the viewpoint.

3   The contours of your face are different on the left and right. So, when compensating for the different heights of your eyebrows, try carefully adding to your eyebrows or trimming the parts that seem too far out of line. Same as eyes, blush, and lips. No face is symmetrical, so adjust the placement and intensity of the colors so that it "looks" symmetrical. Sometimes you have to draw where there is absolutely no eyebrow or lips, and it might feel weird, but that is how you get out of your comfort zone!

4   You can also experiment with changing the thickness and angle of eyeliner or adjust the width of eyeshadow to make your eyes look the same size.

The hardest thing for me when I was first practicing makeup was getting the left and right sides to match. My boss was always telling me off because one eyebrow was higher than the other, or the left side of the lips was different to the right side. Our facial features are almost always asymmetrical. The position of the mouth's corners, the size of eyes, or the height of cheekbones might all be different. Somehow, I couldn't see those differences and I struggled in the beginning. Use this technique to perfect your symmetry.

I remember holding my breath so that my hand wouldn't shake. (And she went on to win the competition!)

I found myself backstage at a gorgeous event I'd only previously seen on TV. And when the show started and the music played, it was like my new life was being celebrated. It gave me the shivers. Even today, I still get tingles up my spine remembering exactly how it felt!

Make your own rules

I bet you think the correct order for makeup is to prepare a base using primer and foundation, draw in eyebrows, then apply eyeshadow. But there's no rule in makeup saying, "You have to do it like this." The key thing is that, when the makeup is finished, the person's best features are brought out and they look great. As long as you remember that, order is secondary at best.

In makeup there are no hard-and-fast steps or rules. If you feel better, that is your answer.

My eyebrows are sparse, so when I want a simple method that amplifies my look, I only have to draw on my eyebrows, and that will be it for me. When I first got my hands on some eyeshadow, it came with a step-by-step set of instructions, but these never seemed to work on my eyes. Here's another example: say today I feel like putting the focus on my lips. I might do those first, then balance my eyebrows and eye makeup to match. What I am saying is that not everybody wants to achieve the same result or has the face for the makeup. I have fun doing my makeup the way I want.

When I'm doing makeup for work, I usually start with the eyes. Many models are surprised. But once the eye makeup is done, I wipe off the eyeshadow fallout with baby wipes, then start the base makeup. I want the under-eye area to be clean, so it's a problem if the dropped eyeshadow makes it look dirty. On the other hand, when I'm not using much eye makeup, I sometimes start with the foundation. See? No rules!

The five precepts of beautiful makeup

While learning makeup in the US, I created my own five precepts of beautiful makeup. Here they are:

1. *Foundation color shall be correct*, unless you want to have different shades on your face and body. You should choose the perfect color, or mix different shades of foundations to create the perfect match; otherwise you look like a Barbie head placed on a different body. Don't choose foundation with the vague thought that "If I apply it thinly it won't matter." And your foundation shouldn't be the same shade as your facial skin tone. Try applying foundation to your collarbone, where it isn't very tanned. If you squint and the foundation is the same color as your collarbone, that's the right shade for you.

2. *Eyeshadow shall be gradient and blended well*, just like the sunset and not a sky with scattered clouds. The eyeshadow should fade out seamlessly, otherwise we will see its patchiness. Try powdering your eyes with loose powder to make it smooth first. The eyeshadow will blend easier that way. Also try moving the brush as softly as if you were tickling the bum of a hamster with a needle. VERY GENTLY!

3. *Lip line shall not be wobbly*. People might start looking at the wobbly lip line and not listen to what you are saying. Lip makeup is often the

last part of the makeup routine, so make sure you don't lose focus here. Smile big and stretch the skin so there are no jumps or wobbliness in the line.

4. *Makeup shall be symmetrical.* Otherwise you can look unbalanced. I've heard it said that "Eyebrows should be sisters, not twins." Yet I still aim for twins, because if you take the time, they can look identical. For the symmetry, try looking at yourself on a cell phone screen; you will be able to see much more in 2D. It can be hard to see the symmetry (or lack thereof) if you are looking in the mirror, because you may be too used to looking at yourself that way.

5. *Makeup should make you look better* and amplify your features. If you look better after washing your face, it's better to go without makeup.

Just as the Buddhist precepts are "suggested," I would not describe any of the above as definitive rules. There are always exceptions. For example, if you are doing goth makeup, the eyeshadow does not have to be blended well. And if you are doing scary makeup, you do not have to look beautiful. If you are playing the Wicked Witch of the East, you will not have to match your foundation color!

People even say, "No makeup is more beautiful than a freshly washed face." That is totally true too; I do not wear makeup on many days. But you can still enjoy learning how to accentuate your features. That's the fun of makeup!

Find the best balance for you.

●

Work on your attitude

My boss taught me more than just the methods and techniques of makeup. She gave me lots of hints about the right attitude and spirit for a professional makeup artist, and how to work responsibly. Not used to working as an assistant, I was always nervous and scared. But my boss told me, "Just do your best. If you do your best no one will complain." In fact, the makeup world is much tougher than you'd expect. Novices in particular are looked on sternly. So the only way to gain acceptance is to show you're doing your best and working your butt off.

When it came to my makeup technique back then, I thought that the natural look was pretty and easy, so I applied almost no foundation on models. But my boss gave me a telling off. "Talk about doing that when you have the skills!" she said. Basically, what she meant was: "You haven't learned how to properly apply foundation yet, so don't talk as if you know about it." And once I started studying foundation properly, I discovered that I didn't even have a basic understanding of good foundation shades. In fact, up to that point I'd been happily focused on studying eye makeup (thanks to my complex about my own eyes).

When I called my pianist mother, she said this: "You might think that the right hand—which plays the melody—is important for the piano, but unless you practice as much on the least prominent sound from your left-hand ring and little fingers, your overall playing won't improve. That's why you should study foundation and all the other parts just as much as eye makeup." I was shocked at how narrow-minded I'd been.

From that day on, I made sketches using photos of my boss's makeup on models, and practiced more on all the other features. In fact, I practised makeup everywhere but the eyes. It was so weird and boring because I love doing eye makeup! But by training this way, I was able to focus on those things that I had avoided before.

Usually I start doing makeup from the eyes, so I would lose my stamina and focus by the time I was applying blush and lips. When I actually focused on these areas, I was able to easily deepen my consideration. Now, I feel like I'm able to see things I couldn't see before. *Why this much foundation? Why do I use this brush, with how much pressure and in what motion?* I can explain my steps logically in a way that others can understand.

Fads, techniques, and little tricks aren't enough to make people beautiful. Only people who have properly studied the fundamentals have the option of saying, "I don't need to do that." Otherwise it is more like, "I don't know how to do that."

Watch out for your attitude, and you will be well on your way to inner as well as outer beauty!

●

Make your beauty truly memorable

I believe that a truly beautiful person is someone who makes other people feel beautiful in themselves.

> "If you meet this person, your emotion will calm down and your heart softens. Even if they have not met them, people will want to meet them."
>
> Jātaka tales

The Venezuelan representative at Miss Universe 2013, Gabriela Isler, was magical! As well as being an outstanding beauty among beauties, she remembered my name. Each time she called out to me—"¡Hola, Kodo!"—I instantly fell under her magic spell. I was the newest and youngest artist back then, and I was doubting if I even deserved to be there and if I could be accepted and welcomed by the team. But to be recognized and remembered by her made me feel that I belonged, and that it was OK for me to be there. I was able to feel proud of my existence. Her calling me by name made me feel so encouraged and my entire experience became unforgettable. I am truly grateful for her kindness. Obviously, Gabriela won the Miss Universe title that year.

I looked at Gabriela and thought: *It's important to be beautiful on the outside, but I want to become the kind of beautiful person that makes others feel beautiful too!*

Nothing lasts forever

Buddhism teaches that life is about impermanence; everything is forever changing. When somebody dies, for example, we really learn this. It can feel surreal and unbelievable to lose somebody that we are so used to.

How to change your perceptions about yourself

You don't have to wait for other people to notice you; you can begin by being kind to yourself. This exercise is like an affirmation. As you know, I used to believe that I was not worthy, and that I was not beautiful. I changed that by talking to myself while gently touching my body and my face—and, yes, I do this naked, with the doors locked!

1   Go somewhere where you feel safe and cannot be disturbed, like your bedroom or bathroom.

2   Stand naked in front of a mirror and look at yourself.

3   Look straight into your eyes.

4   Tell your whole being what it needs to learn, for example:

- I am beautiful
- I am capable
- I am celebrated
- I am loved
- My skin is beautiful
- My body is healthy
- I am free from self-destructive thoughts
- Nobody takes responsibility for my life, so I make my own decisions
- I can grow because I can say no
- I allow myself to receive all that the world has to offer

5 Gently run your hands over your body and face, touching your skin, tapping your head, and letting yourself be aware that this is happening, otherwise your voice can become like background music. Allow your whole body to receive and be in sync with what you are telling it.

6 It may feel totally awkward and crazy to do this, but keep practicing and it will get easier—and, importantly, you will start to believe in yourself!

At first, I was not able to look straight into my eyes when doing this. Then, once I started to feel, "Yeah, that's what I am," I stopped, and I still go back to this exercise from time to time.

I have lost loved ones too. However, my belief is that I don't have to kill them in my mind as well. I imagine that their smile still exists and will live forever. I pretend that these loved ones are still alive in a place far away, and try to live as if they are still alive too. It is too sad to say goodbye to them.

Another way that I approach the impermanence of life is by treating everyone with the knowledge that they will be beyond my reach one day. Every time I get angry at a member of my family, I remind myself that this togetherness is not permanent. I ask myself to remember that and see how I would react. If I continue to be angry, then I allow myself to feel that way; but if I change my feeling, I will act accordingly. Sometimes I imagine, *What if everybody has already left, but are coming back temporarily to see me so that I can appreciate their existence?* This way of thinking allows me to be more grateful.

I sometimes get sad when I remember that life is impermanent, yet this is also a way for me to be grateful and ready for anything that may happen in the future.

●

How to live a "longer" life

In order to live a long life, I have to keep it changing. If there are a lot of changes, my life feels fuller and longer.

I don't like it when every day remains the same. That's because new challenges make life interesting.

I often pause and ask, "What does my heart say?" For example, if I'm in a stable place and seem successful, yet my heart's not excited, it's time to say bye-bye and change my surroundings. Once, my friend told me, "Because you can graduate from things you are familiar with, or attached to, you can keep growing. Some people hesitate to step out of their comfort zone and stability." I think it is a choice, but I am a person who likes to move around like the wind. And the wind dies if it is locked up behind a closed door.

If you don't actively do anything and just go with the flow day after day, time flies past. We're browsing the internet and before we know it, two or three hours have passed. In the blink of an eye, one year, two years, three years of our lives can slip by unnoticed. It's a bit of waste. "Wait, what? Three years have passed?" It feels just like that. Our lives have become shorter and the things we could have experienced during that time haven't been experienced. We've really lost out!

If you're scared of change, your life—the only one you have—can slip by in an instant.

So, if possible, I want to have plenty of experiences and to continue to grow as a person. I want to encounter all sorts of new things. And I want to live my life gradually updating the sense of "this is my style."

In my case, the easiest way to update my style is to travel, like I mentioned in chapters 2 and 3. If possible, visiting a new foreign country is best. But there are plenty of ways to stimulate yourself without traveling anywhere. You can talk with people from different cultures, learn something new, read books from long ago, and experience different cultures through foreign films and documentaries. Don't you agree? When you access a world that's different to your usual one, your life is fun and feels longer. When you look back, I'm sure you'll be content that you used your time fully.

●

When a star is born, there are chemical reactions and disturbances

Feeling agitated and nervous is an opportunity to change yourself. Do something unusual and change your future! You have the ability to take that first step into a brand-new life. If you surpass the struggle of birth, later you might be able to brighten up the world —just like stars do.

When you feel fear, this might be the worst part of the best that is yet to come.

In fact, you should deliberately put yourself into agitating, unsettling, or even fearful situations, because those feelings can change your life. For example, when I decided to go to New York, I was very anxious. I did not know what kind of life would be waiting for me. I would get on the wrong subway trains and get lost many times. Eventually New York became like my backyard, and I had an opportunity to learn makeup surrounded by the best of the best.

When I started training to be a monk, I was not able to keep up with the rituals at first and I felt so embarrassed. It took a while for me to get used to the lifestyle, but I learned the essence of Buddhism, which eventually taught me about equality.

When I decided to come out to my parents, my hands were shaking and so cold. I did not know what kind of reaction I would get from them. I could have been abandoned; that was my worst fear. But now I can talk about my sexuality and have nothing to hide. I became much freer. All these uncomfortable things made me very agitated!

But once I overcame those feelings, I felt like I was setting out on a new road. I guess I'm naturally courageous to take the first step, and I want to share it with you. After spending eight years in New York, I decided to move to Los Angeles because I felt that my growth had stalled. When I had spent a year and a half in Los Angeles, I decided to move because I felt that I was ready to contribute to the Japanese society by talking about LGBTQ+ rights there. Now I am coming back overseas to talk about Buddhism and makeup. You see? My life keeps changing, and that is how I can enjoy a long and rewarding existence.

> Your agitation proves you are internalizing something you're not used to yet. This agitation will enable growth.

●

Be aware of distractions

I know I'm lucky to be living in this age. I didn't have a single friend in high school, but the gay chat room gave me mental support, and it was thanks to the internet that I met my makeup mentor. I appeared on the 2019 Netflix show *Queer Eye: We're in Japan!* for a few minutes, and afterward some international flight attendants recognized me. Even outside Japan people would come up to me and say, "I saw you on *Queer Eye*!" (I'll tell you a little more about that experience in a moment!)

I know that the internet benefits my daily life in various ways and I adore chatting on social media and with friends. Yet I love it so much that once I've turned on a device I'm sometimes sucked in till dawn. As soon as I've turned my smartphone or computer on, I can't stop emailing and chatting. I forget what I want to do and endlessly stare at news, social media, and YouTube. It's my nature. That's why I only look at my smartphone after exercise and lunch. Unless the morning is completely free I won't look at my phone. If I check my notifications, it's over! Before I know it, noon is here, then evening. All my time and any energy for exercise will disappear. That's why I have to be strict with myself: *Make sure this doesn't steal your life, Kodo!* Are social media and other temptations distracting you from your goals?

Having said that, when I'm exercising I do listen to music. I either use a music player that does not have an internet connection, or I turn on airplane mode, and I just play the music or the podcasts that are already downloaded. If I turn off airplane mode, I'd stop myself from achieving my goals. It's a way of dealing with the me who doesn't know when to stop. The more we have things in easy reach—like smartphones and games—the more the rhythm of our life falls apart. If you want to achieve your goals in life, you must firmly grasp the steering wheel so you don't swerve off in some strange direction. Deal with your distractions and keep your focus on what you do want in your life—and that applies to choosing your mentors and role models too, and who you choose to listen to.

I don't mind if you don't like me

One time, when I was 26 years old, I was walking on the Upper West Side, wearing a pair of Emilio Pucci leather heels. Suddenly, a middle-aged man (dressed in gray from head to foot) yelled at me: "Are you a man or a woman?!" It was so unexpected that I couldn't reply. I was shocked.

I was still overwhelmed and upset when I arrived at the café I'd been heading for. It was then that a chic, mature lady wearing a red hat talked to me. "I love your heels!" she said, opening her eyes wide and chatting in French-accented English. "Are those comfortable?"

"Until a goal is realized,
a person must keep on
working. Visualize the scene
of the goal being realized,
and the expectation will
be realized."

Udānavarga, 16:2

I said, "I wouldn't go to Disneyland in these, but I love the shape of them!" Those few words dispelled the sadness I'd been feeling and I had a revelation. I didn't put the shoes on for the man who'd yelled at me. If someone I consider stylish likes my style, that's plenty!

Don't care if just anybody approves of you or not; care if somebody you respect approves of you.

I used to be conscious of people's eyes the instant I stepped outside. But there are people with many different ideas in this world and it's impossible to reach an understanding with everyone. To get where you want to go, you can't listen to absolutely everyone's opinions. I know people might say unpleasant things again—just like that middle-aged man who shouted at me—but now I know to ignore them. I tell myself this: "Don't get distracted by negative people. They might want to step out in heels but they can't! If they did, they wouldn't yell at me." I dress up to go to places where people I admire welcome me. Miss Fame? Billy Porter? Carson Kressley? They would love my heels!

To achieve my dreams, exactly who I ask for advice and what kind of friends I spend time with is very important.

That's because what's around me makes my life. Only ask successful people for advice. Actual achievers won't pour cold water on your dreams. I avoid people who reply to requests for advice with things like, "That's not gonna happen," or, "Only a few people can succeed." Instead, I work hard to meet and talk with those "few people." I don't listen to those people who tried but didn't make it, or who gave up. I personally do not need to learn how they didn't make their dreams come true.

Do you want to succeed in a field you're interested in, but you don't know how? Well, I recommend you consult someone who's been as successful as possible and whom you want to copy, then put yourself somewhere where you can study that person's values up close. Once the high standard becomes your standard, then you are already part of the few people who succeed. A person can only do so much in 24 hours, so the question is how you spend your time and where you put your effort into. I think it has a lot to do with having an optimistic mindset and the ability to visualize success. Thoughts and attitudes are contagious, so always be careful of the company you keep.

Be curious and open-minded

Before I meet someone, I always prepare. I feel the person will be friendlier to me if I'm properly prepared.

When I started doing makeup, I went to all sorts of places to learn techniques: makeup stores, workshops, and tutorial videos. Mostly it was "I know that already!" stuff that didn't answer my many questions. But once I met a makeup artist with true talent who I could respect, I really grew. I don't need makeup advice that consists of marketing gimmicks or quick tricks that only work on certain people. I achieved my dreams by believing only in real, highly polished knowledge and skill. I found people who showed a practical way forward, then applied their successes to my own life, starting with achievable goals.

My favorite quote about an eyeliner from RuPaul's makeup artist is: "People often ask me, 'What makeup products are you using?' But it doesn't matter: as long as it leaves a mark, it works." Groundbreaking! I still have my favorites, but I learned not to depend on the products, but really focus on how I am applying them.

There are precious pieces of advice I received from people whom I truly respect that have opened up my life. For example, I learned that if you follow your passion, money follows. If you chase money, you will have to keep chasing it all your life, whereas if you pursue something that you love, you will be able to earn more, and end up being happier. This is a mentality that I did not have before, but which was taught to me by my Indian friend who works at the World Bank.

Another lesson I learned is this: "Only say yes to jobs that you can perform 100 per cent, otherwise do not take them." I was really awakened by this lesson. It was the Haitian Ambassador to Japan who told me this. I used to take as many jobs as possible, and sometimes I was underprepared or overwhelmed. By having too much on my plate, I was not able to perform 100 per cent at any of my jobs. Once I started to say no, I was able to focus and perform better.

My Spanish friend told me, "You can only grow at a certain speed, so don't rush. In order for a big tree to grow, it needs its time. You cannot rush a plant to grow faster, so don't stress yourself." This advice really saved me from feeling incapable and frustrated.

Ask for help when you need to

My friend who is a Thai designer told me to ask others for help. After all, if you give jobs to other people, you can provide them with an income. It is not wrong to ask for cleaning services or helping hands. She said that it is great to hire help as long as you treat people nicely. In the past I tried to do everything on my own, from mopping to cooking to laundry to doing makeup and cleaning brushes, replying to emails and promoting and negotiating contracts all by myself. I thought that was a virtue and drove myself crazy. However, eventually I gave up and decided to ask for help. I learned that nobody can do everything on their own; we need a professional team to create something bigger. All these teachings were not familiar to me when I was younger. This advice can be a bit intimidating or foreign to some people, but these are lessons I cherish.

Do not try to do everything on your own.

When I first worked with celebrities in LA, I learned that in order for an event or person to make a huge impact, they needed the support of a range of professionals: manager, public relations, social-media manager, fashion stylist, hair stylist, makeup artist, choreographer, dancers, musicians, security, and of course support from family and friends ... the list goes on and on. All the synergy creates a magic and hence a huge impact. I learned that a single person can only do so much after all, and started asking for help without feeling guilty.

If you complain, the problem multiplies

I've mentioned how, when I was training to be a monk
with 90 other novices, if anyone made even a tiny
mistake with the ceremonies or chants, we all had to
start from the beginning. The training was so harsh that
I wanted to run away. Many trainee monks complained
continuously about being scolded by tutors and the
difficulty of the training.

I would join in with those complaints, but later I
tried to step out. Rather than complaining, I turned
my thoughts to the future. *What should I do when the
training is over? What would I eat? What makeup would
I practice?* I wrote those things down in a notebook
and got ready to act on them when the time came. I
could complain, but I couldn't change the contents or
duration of the training. It was much more constructive
to think about what I could do right now. (Shhh, don't
tell anyone—but I even started an imaginary makeup
practice starring statues of Buddha! But it was still
better than complaining.)

You can't control your emotions if you are gripped by
dissatisfaction. In practice, it's impossible to completely
avoid giving voice to complaints and grumbles, but
personally I don't automatically spit out every thought.
It's important to change the angle of the light slightly
and not forget your sense of humor. Things look

differently in different lights and you're the one who controls where to shine that light.

If you always shine a spotlight on your own dissatisfaction, things will be the same wherever you go.

During the Miss Universe international pageant, I once got a call at six in the morning from my boss. She asked me to come and do makeup immediately. *How could you suddenly ask me that so early in the morning?!* I thought. But I looked on the funny side and asked myself this: *Didn't my boss teach me the importance of preparing for anything, because you never know what might happen?* By doing that, I could laugh it off rather than complaining and feeling bad about it later. You don't need to get irritated. It's easier on yourself to laugh and forget bad feelings instead.

Having a hard day? Think of your life as a movie

One time when I was working as a makeup assistant in New York, my boss asked me to go buy eyelashes. "Before leaving for Las Vegas tomorrow," she said, "I want one hundred pairs of black No 18 eyelashes by X brand." Unfortunately, there was only one evening to get them!

I studied a map and worked out a route that would take me around all the drugstores and convenience stores, starting from Times Square in Manhattan. Then I got going ... one store at a time. I was doing well if a store had three sets; I felt totally lucky if they stocked six! Plenty of stores didn't have any and my heart sank each time. I walked around for about four hours but still didn't have a hundred. Meanwhile, the rain started to pour down. I had shopping bags dangling off both arms and I kept thinking, *Well, my boss did say just get as many as I can. Maybe I should give up now?* But when I calmly considered how I'd feel after giving up, I decided I didn't want to have regrets or think, *Why did I give up that time?*

I wasn't doing it begrudgingly just because my boss had asked me. I had decided to do the shopping and I wanted to see it through without giving up. With those thoughts, a little bit of my energy returned. I tried to cheer myself up: *Just pretend you are in* The Devil Wears Prada *movie.* And in the end I went round every store from 40th Street to 70th Street West and East. I got 100 sets! I'd actually done it. *I'm amazing!* I thought (while secretly thinking this experience might end up in a book one day).

But even though I was totally exhausted, I still had to get ready in time for Las Vegas the next day. I took all the fake lashes out of their boxes, bundled them up facing in opposite directions so they wouldn't get crushed, stapled all the receipts together, calculated the total, and sent an email to my boss: "I've done it!"

Many people would probably think, *Why do I have to work so hard?* Instead, take a moment to stop and ask yourself: *How can this experience benefit me?*

When I was in high school, I would feel as lonely as Cinderella, laughed at by her stepmother and stepsisters. The teacher would tell me to study for ten hours every day, and my classmates would make fun of me for my sexuality. Yet I believed that this stress and humiliation could fortify me in the future. I might be a Cinderella covered with ash and feeling hopeless, yet I would still manage to transform into a princess and be happy one day. That little flame of optimism kept me going and I feel like I am able to help people in that situation now. Don't be convinced that you will be covered in ash for life. I believe in working hard, but we also have to be smart and brave enough to say, "Let me try on that glass slipper" when the time comes.

When a glass slipper is handed to you, try it on!

Catch your thoughts as they arise

My favorite way to meditate is to vizualize or verbalize my thoughts so I can clear them out and organize them. This also works when you can't sleep at night.

Our thinking is like a ghost; it comes and goes. So I decided to capture my thoughts on paper in a notebook. It really helps me to organize them. I just keep writing whatever comes to my mind, even about negativity and anger. It is really important to let go of all these emotions.

For example, I might be thinking: *I should go to sleep soon, but I ought to work a bit more. Maybe I can force myself to wake up earlier and go to sleep earlier? But I am very productive at night, so maybe I should set an alarm? I don't want to stop myself working and being productive. Maybe I should go to sleep early and get more things done with a clear mind tomorrow morning?* If I keep thinking these thoughts only in my head, I will never come to a conclusion.

If you cannot see the ghost, it might be worrisome, but if you catch the ghost and make it tangible, it is not really a ghost anymore, right?

Another way is to speak your mind out loud. It makes me feel a bit more resolved and certain, rather than just thinking in my head. Sometimes, I hold my stuffed toy animals and do a voice-over and speak my problems out loud with them. Most of the time, I already know the answer but I cannot face it for some reason. Maybe I just need a moment to pause and reflect, and to postpone taking action.

However, when we really want to solve our problems, I recommend vocalizing or visualizing your thoughts. When I returned to Japan after achieving almost all my dreams, for a while I couldn't find any new goals. I was just spinning my wheels. I was saved by something called "Morning Pages," as introduced in the book *The Artist's Way* by Julia Cameron. I had gotten into the habit of carrying a notebook around with me and just writing down anything: thoughts that popped into my mind, lists of what I wanted to do that day, small goals.

If you can imagine your future goals clearly, you are halfway to making them happen!

Back in Japan, I wrote about how I wanted to get better at Spanish, change my body shape, and improve how I spoke. But when I looked back through my notebook I realized that time was passing without me doing anything about these goals. Meanwhile, my procrastination became obvious and I could give myself a kick in the pants.

I reconsidered why I wanted to improve, thought about which habits I should change to benefit my life, and worked hard to solve those issues. Before reaching for some excuse like "I couldn't do it today either," I thought about the reasons I hadn't been able to do it so far.

How should I use the 24 hours of each day? After writing down my thoughts, I would make "to-do" lists on a separate piece of paper and decide how I would use my day, so I could be productive.

Realizing why you haven't been able to do things and what's hindering you is a shortcut to renewing yourself.

That's why it's useful to record your thoughts each day. Of course there's no need to force yourself when you don't have much energy. I think we need to recharge our batteries before we move forward. Just as a frog crouches right down and gathers its strength before jumping, rest properly when your body feels tired. There's no need to feel guilty when you need to take a break!

Level up before you encounter the boss

You're going to have trouble making good stuff happen if you can't picture it clearly. First, try imagining how you'd like your life to be in the future. I'm always using my imagination and making suitable preparations for the future me. Because I believe that by doing so I can change my future. For example, I imagine how I'll behave after an important job or meeting has gone well and what will be in my bag. I imagine living healthily, surrounded by people and things that spark joy. I spend time imagining all the details of daily life.

If you only make an extra effort when you're facing important people and special occasions, it will be too late! Unless you "level up" in advance, you can't take advantage of opportunities when they come. To lead the life that's your goal, you must collect the items and skills you need and gather people around you. It's just like being the main character in an RPG. Unless you level up in advance, you'll lose the boss fight, and it will be game over. (Not to mention, in real life you can't keep replaying your life over and over like in a video game.)

If you have a dream but have been spinning your wheels for years, it might be that you lack the imagination to make it real. Or perhaps you have shut the door on your dream, thinking, *Such a big dream could never happen.* If you can't imagine it clearly, help yourself through your actions in real life, such as by actually going to the restaurant you pictured yourself in after achieving your dream. Or just order a drink and get a feel for the atmosphere first-hand! If you are applying for a job, go visit the building of your imagined future office, eat at the local cafeteria, and dress up as if you have already been hired. If you want to be a model for an expensive jewelry brand, visit the store and ask to try those jewels on! I have tried on a golden necklace, which I did not buy at the time, but I can still remember the weight and feeling of wearing it, which makes it easier for me to visualize wearing it again ...

However big the dream, you have to make yourself believe it will happen. Unless you've actually seen the goal line, you can't imagine it, can you? I have my weak moments too, but I know I need to believe in myself. If you can imagine it, the dream is halfway to happening!

Imagine all of your dreams have come true, and let's celebrate already!

One of my favorite books is *The Secret* by Rhonda Byrne in which she explains the Law of Attraction. I would highly recommend it! Basically, it says to start living as if your dreams have already come true. When I was in New York, for example, I really wanted to work for a makeup artist and join the makeup team

Ice cream magic

I would like to share a version of the Law of Attraction that I came up with and called "ice cream magic."

1   That first taste of ice cream makes you fabulously happy, doesn't it? Try superimposing that feeling of happiness onto the successful you of the future, and visualize the feeling of your dreams already coming true, such as: "Many people appreciated my book!" Taste a little of the pleasure you get when a dream comes true.

2   Now enjoy the second spoon: "My first safari holiday was so exciting." And the third: "I have become fluent in Spanish!" Make sure you phrase it as if it has already happened.

3   You can superimpose your dreams onto everyday moments of happiness, like that "Aaaah ..." when you enter the bath or that "Mmmm ..." when you feel a refreshing breeze.

And here's a special version: "The Dinner to Celebrate Dreams Come True." Go to a fabulous restaurant with your favorite friends in real life. Choose somewhere a little nicer than where you usually go, as if to reward yourself. Now order courses and desserts to share. Then, as you taste each dish, take turns to talk about the pleasure you feel after achieving a dream. It should be as if your dreams have come true and you are looking back at the past while having a celebratory meal.

I did this with my Spanish friends a few years back. For the first dish I said, "OMG. I've appeared on the *Queer Eye* show!" Then I took a bite and tasted both the pleasure of the food and the achievement.

"How have people reacted?" my friend asked.

"I got lots of messages of congratulations! And that led to me appearing in *Vogue*!" I said.

The more concrete details you give about your dreams actually happening, the more real they feel. Together, pretend that your wishes have actually come true and share your blessings. Imagining the future together will bring your dreams closer to reality, don't you think?

And there's more to this story. When you live like your dreams have come true, they really do! Several years later I actually did appear on *Queer Eye*! And I really was interviewed by *Vogue*! When they contacted me, I was so shocked.

So how about it? Surely it's worth a try?

of Miss Universe. I would write in a notebook, "I could be an assistant to a makeup artist and work for Miss Universe," hundreds of times and I would chant and visualize the situation. I have done this with many goals, and almost all of them have come true! (Except for romantic relationships, as *The Secret* says, trying to change somebody else's life does not work ... which I should have known way earlier!)

●

Believe your dreams can come true

Being on the Netflix show *Queer Eye* was a dream come true for me.

When I was in middle school, I came across the original series *Queer Eye for the Straight Guy* on FOX channel. I was so surprised that there were openly gay men appearing on the TV. When I was young, I watched a lot of anime and in those anime, gay people were usually depicted as perverted villains. However, in *Queer Eye*, they were the heroes helping heterosexual people. How could they come out and not be discriminated against in public? I was so curious. But then they were only helping others and being kind, so what was there to blame them for, right?

Later, when I started working for Miss USA and Miss Universe, I met one of the original cast of *Queer Eye*, Carson Kressley, who is also a judge on *RuPaul's Drag Race*. He was a fashion commentator on the Miss USA and Miss Universe shows too. My boss assigned me to help Carson—how surreal! I was able to do his makeup for him each time he appeared during the production. He was kind enough to mail me an autographed book of his. He was such a fun and smart professional who paid attention to what the people around him were talking about, and would instantly reflect back with the funniest jokes.

Later, as I got more speaking opportunities in Japan as an LGTBQ+ activist, somebody who had come to one of my events contacted me about *Queer Eye* coming to Japan. He was Kan, who was to star in the episode "Crazy in Love," and he asked if he could introduce me to the producers of the show. First, I auditioned to be the ambassador role, and I was not selected. Second, I went into the interview to work as a hair and makeup artist, but I was not selected. I was saddened, yet I took it as my destiny, hoping that I could somehow turn things around. Then the producers emailed me, saying that they had the perfect role for me, and that is how I ended up being on the show.

The episode was shot in a park in Shinjuku. The series host, Karamo Brown, and I met beforehand

and I was told that I would surprise Kan. The topic that we talked about was something very close to my heart as well. Kan told me how when he was studying in the UK, he felt discriminated against in the gay community when he was told "No Asians" on the dating apps, and he also felt excluded by the Japanese community where they made fun of gay people, calling them faggots. Karamo said that he was discriminated against because of his dark skin, so he has to tell himself: "Someone may not like me, but I like myself."

Appearing on *Queer Eye* marked a huge change in my life. I was recognized in the supermarket in Atlanta, at Disney World in Florida, and even inside a restroom in Thailand. (In the restroom, there were no paper towels, and I didn't have a handkerchief, and a security guard who recognized me talked to me right when I was about to flick my hands real hard!) It is startling to be recognized, but I am grateful that my message is now being heard. This is why I will keep fighting for the right to live as we want to live, and to be who we want to be.

I know that people have their own preferences and tastes, and some people are fortunate enough to be considerate of the feelings of others and some not. I refuse to be made sad or angry by people who are not able to know me for who I really am. I might not always be proud of my body or capabilities, but I love my true self; my will to be considerate and courageous. My inner being is something that will not change over time.

> **No matter what people say, as long as you protect the little flame of self-validation in your heart, it will not be blown out.**

Even if other people deny your light, don't let the fire go out. I am here to protect your light too! Picture your life with vision boards.

When I was in New York, I met many models. What surprised me was that some of the models used their own photo as their mobile screen wallpaper. I said to myself, *How self-absorbed!* But you know what? What is wrong with loving yourself? I started to question why I would think they were vain. It could be how I was raised and taught that we are not supposed to talk proudly of ourselves—but today those values are "old medicine." Yes, some people might go overboard, but there are also those of us who start to believe that they are not worthy, which was the case for me.

Now that I think about it, maybe the models truly loved themselves, loved the photos, or maybe it was a way to remind and encourage themselves that they are beautiful and worthy of great opportunities. Whatever the case may be, I was inspired. Since then, I started to set something on my mobile home screen that I used to think was too big for me, such as an advertisement for *Queer Eye*. I put it on my phone so that I could keep seeing it every single day, until I would forget that I once thought this big program was just out of my reach. The moment I had forgotten about my intention, I was cast to be a part of the show.

It is not a sin to love and prioritize yourself.

Same as publishing a book in English! I put an image of a particular publisher's logo on my screen, and now I am working with them.

It is also a good idea to use this method for your laptop wallpaper, or print photos of what you wish for and put them in a place that you constantly see. The key is to get used to it, and your perception toward the image changes. What used to seem out of reach can come up close.

I also do this with business cards, and whenever I meet somebody who I've wanted to meet for a while, I display their business card. I have a shelf where

I display my favorite objects that spark joy, such as souvenirs from favorite destinations or photos of me with my best friend. So I place the business cards on that shelf. Usually I get contacted by them later or have another opportunity to meet them. When I move on to a different ambition, I put up the card of who I want to connect more with. This is how I was able to meet people who helped pave my way.

It is not a scientific approach, but I feel that "changing what is normal to me" is the key to achieving more. When you believe that you can, you convince destiny!

People are like pens

I think that people are a little like pens. We all come in different sizes, forms, and colors. Some of us might be pencils, markers, crayons, or even fountain pens. Some pens might draw bold lines; others might draw fine lines. Some might be black, yellow, or multicolored. It really comes down to what we decide to draw. It might be an illustration, a story, a poem, or a comic.

I think we should always learn how the thickness of our pen works, and how the colors can be best used. There is a time when boldness is needed, and other times when we need a thin line to deliver something delicate. There is no better or worse in any pen, and we can all do unique things. There is no waste, and we are all capable.

Let's utilize our ink and have fun before it runs out ...

Let your true colors shine

When I was little, I loved the colors yellow and purple. It was because I thought "neutral" colors suited me, neither blue for boys nor pink for girls.

I've experienced the world through a multi-gendered spirit, so I can relate both to men and women. I am gifted to see an individual as who they are, and I can communicate with them as Kodo, someone who doesn't have to limit himself to have a specific gender identity. I think my existence is freeing for others.

I mentioned right at the start of this book how I came across a description for this gender identity I've been granted: "gender gifted." I love those words and want others to use them to describe me. "Gifted" suggests talent and being blessed. When I realized that being different enabled me to do and understand things others couldn't, I was able to love myself more. Meanwhile, enduring ridicule from others has made me stronger and more thoughtful. Memories of being treated as inferior serve as a limitless supply of fuel that powers my whole life.

Because you are unique, you could be the missing piece to complete the puzzle.

We all have many obstacles in our lives. But I want you to realize that those challenges and the things we've endured can turn into superpowers that help us later.

Let's think in colors! When yellow joins blue and red in the world, orange and green can be born for the first time. And when blue and red combine to create purple, a bridge can be made between red and blue. Our unique characteristics are sources of new possibilities and hope. There must be something that only I can do because I feel both male and female—purple; and yet I am neither fully male nor fully female—yellow. This concept has validated my existence.

When each person shines with their own colors, the world is more vibrant and beautiful. Just like a puzzle piece. We are unique, so we can fill the gaps in society. There is beauty in being a person who is authentic.

Finally

This happened to me recently: I called up a friend from when I was 18 and lived in Boston. He's an American guy that I used to hang out with, but we hadn't spoken for more than a decade. I knew that I was attracted to men back then, yet my friend told me I was so scared to say the word "gay" that I'd only make the shape with my lips. I actually did that! I'd completely forgotten.

Now I do interviews for magazines and TV programs. I show my face, state my name, say I'm homosexual, and smile. Even I'm surprised. That conversation made me suddenly realize how much my attitude had changed. Obviously, I much prefer the way I am now to when I was 18. I can be the real me instead of hiding things and living in fear.

I wanted to believe that being a homosexual was not wrong, but I needed to have conviction. I needed to believe it myself. It took a long journey until I started meeting people who tried their best to convince me to come out, and who told me to wear makeup and heels and go out. I studied LGBTQ+ history through various movies, TV shows, books, and conversations. I pondered on why I was infested with ideas that homosexuality was wrong. I then joined the monk training and I was encouraged and validated in my sexuality by Buddhism. I know that going places, meeting people, and learning information are the keys to convincing yourself that you deserve to be treated equally and with respect.

After all, I understand that everybody is equal, regardless of any differences between people. Race, skills, gender, wealth, status, etc.—none of these matter. What matters is our awareness and intention. It is my role to help people realize that we are all equal no matter what.

Do not be deceived by anybody or anything trying to tell you that you are less than them.

This is something that I continue to ask myself often: *How do I want to live? How shall I spend my time on this earth?* Because I am homosexual, I am not going to marry a woman I love and have children. I see people around me with growing families and I ask myself, *What's my purpose as a living being?* Even now, I sometimes feel sad before I fall asleep. But there's one meaning to my life I'm absolutely sure of ... and that's encouraging others. Touching hope-filled hearts makes me happier than anything.

Something else I think about before sleep is, *How can I live happily?* There was a particular day, before I came out to my parents, when my heart spoke: "Now I've experienced this day, I'll never regret anything." I'd spent the day with my Spanish best friend, in a place where I could be open about my sexuality. I was in Barcelona, and we were walking along the beach, with a pink and purple sunset, and our conversation bloomed like flowers into so much laughter. The temperature, wind, and time of day felt memorably welcoming. I just needed to be who I was. I did not have to hide, or do anything else. Everything felt perfect and abundant. *With days like this in my life*, I thought, *I don't need honor, money, power, or beauty. What could bring more happiness than enjoying many moments of fun and laughter? I wouldn't even need a long life. That moment I can be 100 per cent myself, that is the happiest feeling ever.*

> "A victory that can be overturned is not a real victory. A victory that cannot be overturned is the true victory."
>
> Jātaka Tales

●

Let's fight discrimination by celebrating ourselves

I think hate only creates hate. So how can we overcome discrimination and promote inclusivity?

When I was in Los Angeles, I went to see a Halloween parade in West Hollywood, where there are countless gay bars. There were some people who were protesting against homosexuality. They were behind a secluded barricade put up by the police for security. They quoted phrases loaded with faith-based values and made threatening slurs, such as "Repent or perish." There was so much hate toward the people who were marching in costumes, especially LGBTQ+ people.

What happened was that I started to see people stopping in front of the protesters, and yelling back with hate. They were arguing brutally. It was painful for me to witness this sight. Why would people come here just to spread hate? Why did anyone have to yell back? It was scary and filled me with negative thoughts. Then all of a sudden the DJ for the Halloween parade put on a famous gay anthem, and lots of people started singing loudly. The crowd turned to face the DJ and started dancing crazily to this, their favorite song. The protesters were completely ignored. The hateful voices lost their power because the people in the parade were having so much fun and did not pay attention to them anymore. Wow, what a way to fight back, right?

The message I got is: "We do not care what you think; we are too happy out here to pay attention to you." I felt that the best way to fight the discrimination was to demonstrate how much fun we could have, and almost make people want to join the party, because it looked that happy. People just walked away from the hateful protest and the protesters soon seemed to be doing something for nothing.

I believe that there is a way to triumph without hate. Of course, I still get angry when I see something discriminatory, but I have learned that anger only hurts me. So how about we use art, such as music, dance, design, makeup, fashion, entertainment, and other forms of culture, to celebrate diversity instead? When I first watched movies such as *Paris is Burning* and *The Adventures of Priscilla, Queen of the Desert* I realized that I was not the only one suffering. While I enjoyed the

"There is no discrimination
in Love."

Jātaka Tales

makeup and the performances, I was also empowered and educated by what I saw on screen.

Today, I want to use art as an agent to promote diversity. When something is fun, beautiful, and entertaining, it is easier to learn. If we force people to study hate crimes or suicide rates, it is not always going to work because it is not fun. Nobody wants to be forced to learn about something saddening or upsetting. They might say something back such as, "That is also happening outside the LGBTQ+ community," or "I don't think it is relevant to me," so I think there is huge hope in something inviting and fun.

That is why I use makeup. Makeup can be appreciated globally, and it engages people. Also by showcasing myself in makeup, I can update stereotypes of monks, and offer hope that we can all be free. And I can encourage people by doing makeup, letting them know that we can all feel beautiful. When I do makeup on somebody, they often start to share their vulnerabilities with me as well. I would love to keep using makeup as a tool to reach people's hearts and listen to their stories. I would love to connect people from different backgrounds and let them know that, deep inside, we are all the same, experiencing the same sufferings and wanting the same things. I might use the ancient teachings of Buddhism and trendy makeup products, but I am using them both in the same spirit.

The circle of life

Be yourself and find someone who understands
you. When nothing else matters except that you are
accepted for your true self, for me, that's the key to a
happy life. Throughout life, happiness and suffering
arise again and again. But all things must pass.

Changes might come that you can't even imagine
now. Even when everything is going well, it might
suddenly go wrong. Yet turn that around and think
about it: life is impermanent. Unfortunately, there will
be tragedies and problems in the future, yet I want to
always choose to look up, be positive, and unite people
to stand up for a peaceful world.

DISCOVER MORE INSPRATIONAL STORIES
PUBLISHED BY WATKINS

Living and Loving in the Age of AIDS by Derek Frost

A compelling, heart-rending and uplifting memoir about one couple's love story through the AIDS epidemic. Derek Frost, a skilled designer and photographer, met and fell in love with Jeremy Norman in 1977. Together they started Aids Ark, a charity that has saved thousands of lives.

The Joyful Environmentalist by Isabel Losada

A feel-good book for everyone who loves our planet and is looking for solutions. Fast, funny and inspiring. This book assures readers that there is plenty they can do and that their efforts really *will* make a difference, whilst making them laugh throughout.

Saltwater in the Blood by Easkey Britton

A powerful piece of feminist nature writing by the pioneer of women's big-wave surfing in Ireland. Easkey Britton provides a female perspective on surfing and the mental skills required, as well as the need to respect and value the ocean.

Discover more at www.watkinspublishing.com

WATKINS
Sharing Wisdom
Since 1893

DISCOVER MORE INSPRATIONAL STORIES PUBLISHED BY WATKINS

<u>Enough</u> by Jessica Rose Williams

Despite what the media may tell us, we are not what we buy or what we own. Williams shares her personal transformation to show how you can live an intuitive, minimal life, with a unique style of your own.

<u>The Path to Healing is a Spiral</u> by Anna McKerrow

From screaming in a grey industrial estate, to sobbing along to Elton John with a room full of strangers, to gong baths, reiki and angel healing, Anna McKerrow has tried everything to make sense of her grief. And somewhere on her long journey she found her way to real self-understanding and healing.

<u>F*cked at 40</u> by Tova Leigh

A funny, raw and empowering mid-life-crisis-with-a-difference, vlogger, mother, lover businesswoman and social media phenomenon Tova Leigh explores what the hell you are supposed to do when you find yourself living a life you don't remember signing up for.

Discover more at www.watkinspublishing.com

WATKINS
Sharing Wisdom
Since 1893

WATKINS
Sharing Wisdom
Since 1893

The story of Watkins began in 1893, when scholar of esotericism John Watkins founded our bookshop, inspired by the lament of his friend and teacher Madame Blavatsky that there was nowhere in London to buy books on mysticism, occultism or metaphysics. That moment marked the birth of Watkins, soon to become the publisher of many of the leading lights of spiritual literature, including Carl Jung, Rudolf Steiner, Alice Bailey and Chögyam Trungpa.

Today, the passion at Watkins Publishing for vigorous questioning is still resolute. Our stimulating and groundbreaking list ranges from ancient traditions and complementary medicine to the latest ideas about personal development, holistic wellbeing and consciousness exploration. We remain at the cutting edge, committed to publishing books that change lives.

DISCOVER MORE AT:

www.watkinspublishing.com

Sign up to
our newsletter

Keep up to date
with our events

Find out
about new releases

We celebrate conscious, passionate, wise and happy living.

Be part of that community by visiting:

 watkinspublishing   watkinspublishing

 @watkinswisdom   @watkinswisdom   @watkinspublishing